Bob and Helen Kleberg of King Ranch

4

Bob and Helen Kleberg of King Ranch

BY HELEN KLEBERG GROVES

WRITTEN AND RESEARCHED WITH BILL BENSON

PHOTO CREDITS

Ernest Graham front cover, back cover

Toni Frissell Plates 3, 5, 6, 51, 52, 56, 60, 61, 70, 71, 72, 73, 74, 75, 77, 79, 80, 81, 82, 84, 88, 89, 90, 97, 98, 102, 103, 104, 105, 107, 108, 110, 111, 112, 114, 115, 117, 118, 126, 127; Pages 86 (bottom), 120 (bottom), 134, 158 (top), 213 (top), back fly sheet

Helen C. Kleberg front fly sheet; Plates 1, 4, 46, 47, 48, 49, 50, 53, 54, 55, 57, 59, 62, 63, 64, 65, 68, 69, 76, 85, 86, 87, 94 (bottom left and bottom right), 95, 96, 99, 106, 109, 113, 121, 128, 129, 136, 138, 140, 142, 143, 144, 147, 150, 151, 152, 153, 154, 155, 156, 157, 158; Pages 20 (bottom), 76 (bottom), 86 (top), 98, 99, 110, 111 (bottom), 112 (bottom), 135, 186, 199 (top), 214, 240, 241, 242, 244, 264 (top)

BRIGHT SKY PRESS
Box 416
Albany, Texas, 76430

10   9   8   7   6   5   4   3   2   1

Library of Congress Cataloging-in-Publication Data

Groves, Helen Kleberg, 1927-
   Bob and Helen Kleberg of King Ranch / by Helen Kleberg Groves; written and researched with Bill Benson.
      p. cm.
   Includes bibliographical references (p.).
   ISBN 1-931721-38-6 (alk. paper)
1. Kleberg, Robert Justus, 1896-1974. 2. Kleberg, Helen Campbell, 1902-1963. 3. Ranchers—Texas—Biography. 4. Ranchers' spouses—Texas—Biography. 5. Ranch life—Texas—History. 6. King Ranch (Tex.)—History. I. Benson, Bill, 1943- II. Title.

SF194.2.K59G76 2004
338.7'636213'092--dc22

2003069705

Design by DJ Stout and Erin Mayes, Pentagram, Austin, TX

Printed in China through Asia Pacific Offset

It is with great affection
that I pass this family story of my loving parents
on to my children and grandchildren

Contents

Foreword

ANNE AND TOBIN ARMSTRONG

We take great pride in being able to share a few of our memories of Bob and Helen Kleberg and King Ranch, and above all to be a small part of the memoirs of our lifelong friend, Helenita Kleberg Groves. Life on a Texas ranch has its obvious satisfactions: working with the land, with animals, and with cowboys. However, the nonrancher might be surprised to learn that, at least on the Armstrong Ranch in the brush country south of Corpus Christi, one of our greatest joys has been our social life. Yes, your nearest neighbor may live many miles away—but what neighbors! What big-hearted, strong-minded, passionate people. Extraordinary people like Bob and Helen Kleberg.

During the near half-century that Bob ran King Ranch, a person could say, without fear of exaggeration, that he was the public face of Texas ranching and therefore of Texas itself. He appeared on the cover of *Time* and was profiled at great length in *Fortune*. Will Rogers, a family friend of the Klebergs, wrote about Bob and the ranch in his newspaper column.

When Edna Ferber decided she wanted to write a novel about an imposing Texas rancher, she came calling at King Ranch. She and Bob did not hit it off, to put it mildly, and she was not able to base her famous, and in many quarters infamous, book directly on the Klebergs. Still, the couple at the center of the novel—he the lifelong cowboy, she the horse-loving daughter of the eastern establishment—did in fact bear more than a passing resemblance to Bob and Helen.

Besides their renown as ranchers, they were genuine celebrities in the world of Thoroughbred racing. Master breeder that he was, Bob saw his horse Assault win the Triple Crown a mere twelve years after he bought his first Thoroughbred. Bob and Helen moved as easily in the glamorous world of horse racing as they did through the South Texas mesquite. Being joined in the Winner's Circle by Bob Hope or President Eisenhower came as naturally to them as did sleeping in the open with their loyal and splendid cowboys, the Kineños.

So yes, Bob and Helen Kleberg were extraordinary people, as everyone knew. We had the tremendous fortune to know them well, and our lives remain so very enriched by the memories they left us.

We'll never be able to say in this short space how much these two meant to Texas and to us. We can only give a glimpse of what it was like to be their friends.

Tobin knew them longest, so his story will come first.

TOBIN ARMSTRONG

The Armstrong Ranch was neighbor to what was then Santa Gertrudis Ranch, and my uncle, Tom Armstrong, was Bob's best friend. Bob and Tom had the wonderful custom of spending their Decembers camping and hunting in the Los Amigos Camp in the Norias section of Bob's ranch. They brought their families along, and the affair always became a first-class safari. You'd have ladies' tents, men's tents, and visitors' tents. And visitors came from all over to enjoy the legendary Kleberg hospitality.

Among them were heads of industry, movie stars, Rockefellers, and six-year-old boys like me. I opened gates and performed other terrifically important tasks for Uncle Tom and Bob, trying to make myself useful so I could stay out there with them.

Those men were my heroes. They knew how to have fun. In fact, with Bob, nothing was ever drudgery. When it came time to perform some routine ranching

Bob Kleberg Jr. and Anne and Tobin Armstrong

task, he'd find a way of making it sound like an adventure. Instead of saying, "We have to go check on that water well," he'd say, "Let's go see if that turkey flock is back." He had a great imagination and saw everything in bright colors.

If he could make checking the water level in a well exciting, imagine what he could do with a safari. He and my Uncle Tom were also extremely competitive. You never knew when one would pull the hunting car over and challenge the other to some kind of trick shot.

Bob carried his love of competition indoors. I visited the Klebergs regularly as I got older. Every time I went to see him, he'd have a magazine article set aside that I'd have to read right away and then be prepared to debate. But, even though he had such a strong personality, I never had to agree with Bob. He just liked to argue, to exercise his mind. Of course, Bob would never admit that he was wrong, but that's another story.

Helen was a beautiful woman with a lovely soft voice and a deeply felt love of art and beauty. She was also a great rider, a great shot, and a great hunter. When she died, she chose to be buried next to her favorite fishing hole.

I continued to learn from Bob and Helen as the decades passed. Bob got me involved in the fight he helped lead against the potentially devastating foot-and-mouth disease and in his push to achieve a more accurate grading system for beef. I learned so much about ranching, and life, under his guidance.

ANNE ARMSTRONG

I met the Klebergs through their daughter, Helenita. We were roommates together at Foxcroft, near Middleburg, Virginia. From her I heard these wonderful stories about life on a great Texas ranch. I was so excited when she invited my sister and me to visit.

The ranch was a foreign world to a girl from Louisiana, but I loved it right away. I went on roundups with Helenita, and we bathed in cattle troughs and just generally had a wonderful time.

I was swimming in the Klebergs' pool one hot summer day when I met Tobin.

Bob and Helen made life so wonderful for us. Their guests and their hospitality were always so exciting.

Helen Kleberg was a calming influence on Bob and never stole the spotlight. We will never know how much influence she had on all of the wonderful things he accomplished. She never bragged and continuously supported him. She was a lady through and through. To anyone who would meet Bob, Tom Armstrong, Johnny Kenedy, or the younger ones, they might say, "Ah, these wild and woolly Texans, they are a rough, tough lot." They were stopped in their tracks, however, when they met Helen; there was no one more elegant. She was never flamboyant and was a heck of a shot. She had the most beautiful voice I have ever heard in my life and was every inch a lady. She learned everything Bob knew and was always at his side. She was a wonderful mother.

Bob was the most resilient human being I have ever met. He would have a late-night party and you would think he needed a little sleep. Well, he would be up at dawn and he would do everything the cowboys did and then some.

With their love of life, hard work, and excellence, Bob and Helen represented what makes us most proud of Texas—and America. When I became ambassador to St. James Court, years after both of them had died, I met so many people whose lives had been touched by Bob and Helen. The Queen Mother was just crazy about Bob, and she talked about him often. Having an association with the Klebergs, and with King Ranch, gave me quite a calling card in England, a country the Klebergs deeply loved.

Please enjoy this precious book.

Introduction

As I look back on my life, I feel fortunate for growing up under the influence of my mother and father, Helen Campbell Kleberg and Bob Kleberg. They established principles of respect and loyalty that remain with me to this day. Much of what they taught me had been passed down from their forefathers.

Daddy's tenacity of purpose, combined with his love of animals, nature, and independence, inspired him to travel a path unknown to others. He attended college for only a short time, but the world became his classroom. He studied the secrets of genetics and carefully noted ways to create a new breed of cattle, the Santa Gertrudis, as well as the unique King Ranch remuda and one of the greatest Thoroughbred racehorses in the world. Daddy revered his responsibilities as a steward of land and livestock no matter where he was in the world.

He was a visionary who convinced others to follow as he pursued his dream of providing a source of meat protein to underdeveloped foreign lands. His inventive mind was spurred by a powerful spirit of self-determination. Daddy used to say that bad training ruined more people, horses, and dogs than if you just pointed them in the right direction and let them train themselves. I believe strongly in that principle, in guiding

Helen C. Kleberg and Bob Kleberg Jr., December 25, 1946, at Dick and Mary Lewis Kleberg's house, built by Bessie Yoakum Larkin

but not laying it all out. I said to him one time, "Oh, so-and-so is getting old. When he retires, who is going to be head of the cow outfit?" Daddy said, "The leader will emerge. Don't trouble yourself."

Daddy also used to say, "Show me someone who tells me they're going to make a lot of money and I'll tell you they won't. You show me someone who wants to do something, accomplish something, and they'll do well if they work at it." A keen observer, he possessed an unquenchable thirst for knowledge. He taught me to widen my vision, to not just look straight ahead but to try to see a bigger picture because things come at you from every angle. His wonderful accomplishments reflect his firm belief that "life is an expression of what you are." Although his faith in God was strong, he seldom went to church. The vaqueros begged him to go on Easter Sunday so it would rain—one rare event leading to another.

My mother could draw from a rich store of experiences and education. This came from classrooms, the halls of our nation's Capitol, and the offices and homes of this country's great business, industrial, educational, military, and political leaders. She learned the protocol demanded of a congressman's daughter and was a gracious hostess. She loved horses and the outdoors. Her strong spirit of independence, matched by an uncompromising drive for perfection in whatever she did, was reinforced by her abiding admiration for my father, thus bringing out the best in both of them. They were a marvelous pair and complemented each other perfectly. Wherever they traveled, they won the hearts of many. Entertained on ranches or in cities, they were quick to reciprocate.

My mother said, "Worrying is a totally worthless thing to do. You either do something about it, if you can, or you forget it and go on with your life." She also used to say, "If you don't have respect, you don't have anything." She taught me to speak "properly" and to treat everyone the same — with respect and good manners, whether I liked them or not.

My parents taught me through their actions and words to hold firmly to honesty, integrity, and love of country. They always voted, and they taught me to do the same. They sought new opportunities and learned new things. I don't think they had a selfish bone in their bodies. They collaborated on just about everything, working closely all their lives.

My grandparents came from Protestant families who had worked land and livestock and prized education. Mother and Daddy's fathers were both educated in and had practiced law. Hospitality was a grand tradition in the King, Kleberg, and Campbell families, and it was a constant in my parents' home or camp. Cattle buyers, royalty, top military officials, neighbors, friends, artists, and writers all sat at our table. My parents were always concerned for the welfare of family, friends, and employees. They taught me that loyalty and respect for our nation was number one, with Texas not far behind.

For most of us, destiny chooses an individual to contribute significantly to our lives, but even more remarkable is when individuals from several generations give so much and influence so many. As a descendent of such a wonderful and rare legacy, I am privileged to help preserve my parents' life stories.

It is with great affection that I pass this family history on to my children: Helen, Emory, John, Caroline, Henrietta, and Dorothy. It gives me joy to know that they are abiding by their great-grandfather Robert Justus Kleberg's dictum: "Those who possess power, property, or influence must hold it in trust for the use of their fellow man."

It is my hope that my children add their lives' dreams and achievements to this legacy to be passed on to their children and their children's children.

ACKNOWLEDGMENTS

There are so many people I want to thank. It would be impossible to name them all.

First must be my parents and theirs, for well-kept journals, letters, photographs, articles, and clippings— and the incredibly diverse and active interests they pursued. A wealth of untapped material resides in their collections.

Next I want to thank the family, Kineños, and friends on the ranch and around the world.

I am also grateful for the work of old and new friends who have helped gather the tales, quotations, and photographs for this book.

On roundup there is camaraderie, the team effort that makes the work come to fruition. So it is with a book—each day, each book, and each life is part of God's larger pattern.

HELEN KLEBERG GROVES

Family Tree

Captain Richard King
JULY 10, 1824—APRIL 14, 1885

Henrietta Chamberlain
JULY 21, 1832—MARCH 31, 1925

MARRIED
DECEMBER 10, 1854

Henrietta Maria King
APRIL 17, 1856—
APRIL 1918

Ella Morse King
APRIL 13, 1858—
AUGUST 28, 1900

Richard King II
DECEMBER 15, 1860—
SEPTEMBER 27, 1922

Alice Gertrudis King
APRIL 29, 1862—
JULY 13, 1944

Robert Justus Kleberg Sr.
DECEMBER 5, 1853—
OCTOBER 10, 1932

Robert E. Lee King
FEBRUARY 22, 1864—
MARCH 1, 1883

MARRIED
JUNE 17, 1886

Richard M. Kleberg
NOVEMBER 18, 1887—MAY 8, 1955

Henrietta Rosa Kleberg
(Larkin, Armstrong)
JULY 17, 1889—OCTOBER 24, 1969

Alice Gertrudis Kleberg
(East)
JANUARY 9, 1893—SEPTEMBER 6, 1997

Philip Pitt Campbell
April 25, 1862—May 26, 1941

Mary Helen Goff
December 9, 1869—May 3, 1961

Married
November 23, 1892

**Dorothy Campbell
(Killmaster)**
September 4, 1893—
September, 1979

Colin Campbell
November 23, 1895—
July 26, 1970

**Elizabeth Campbell
(Wright)**
July 18, 1898—
March 1983

Robert J. Kleberg Jr.
March 29, 1896—October 13, 1974

Helen Campbell
April 4, 1902—June 12, 1963

**Sarah Spohn Kleberg
(Johnson, Shelton)**
April 12, 1898—May 20, 1942

Married
March 2, 1926

**Helen King Kleberg
(Alexander, Groves)**
October 20, 1927

Kings and Klebergs

Texas beginnings at the time of the great trail drives
and the emergence of the Texas livestock industry

"Buy land and never sell…"

CAPTAIN KING

Richard King, my great-grandfather, son of Irish immigrants, was born on July 10, 1824, in Orange County, New York. As a young orphan, he was apprenticed to a jeweler in New York City. His duties consisted mostly of sweeping and babysitting, which he despised. Not finding babysitting to his liking, he stowed away on the *Desdemona*, bound for Alabama. Soon discovered, he became cabin boy for the kindly captain, who later sent young Richard to his family in New England to be educated. After one winter there, King returned to river life in the South, where he became a skillful riverboat pilot.

Around 1845, his friend Mifflin Kenedy, a Quaker from Downington, Pennsylvania, asked King to join him in piloting riverboats on the Rio Grande for the U.S. Army. As the Mexican War loomed, Fort Brown and Brownsville were being built across from Matamoros, Mexico. King and Kenedy became friends with Charles Stillman, who had a riverboat and pack train, as well as with the Yturria family and a young Army officer named Robert E. Lee. Lee advised King to "buy land and never sell."

In 1847, after the war, King and Kenedy became partners, hauling freight on the river with Army surplus boats and other vessels they ordered in Pennsylvania, where excellent yellow pine was available for construction. River trade was active as adventurers provisioned for travel to the California gold fields. In addition to his river business, King did some bartending and innkeeping.

One day King, angry and weary, shouted a stream of profanity when he discovered a houseboat occupying his regular mooring. A slender young woman dressed him down in no uncertain terms for his language in the presence of a lady. Henrietta Chamberlain was standing on the deck of the houseboat belonging to her father, the Rev. Hiram Chamberlain. King apologized and came to the Reverend's sermons so he could meet this feisty young lady.

About 1852, King, who was now captain of his ship, rode horseback with friends over the open prairies from Brownsville to Corpus Christi to see the new port and the Lone Star State Fair. The fair failed to impress him, but the tall grass, deer, antelope, and particularly the land captured his imagination. Around 1853, King purchased substantial acreage within a Spanish land grant, the Rincón de Santa Gertrudis, situated forty-five miles southwest of Corpus Christi in the forks formed by the Santa Gertrudis and San Fernando Creeks. On December 10, 1854, he married Henrietta in a ceremony performed by her father in Brownsville. They honeymooned camping out on their new ranch, where the Captain taught Henrietta to shoot the pistol and rifle he had given her. She kept her weapons and her Bible close by for the rest of her life.

HIRAM AND HENRIETTA

Henrietta's father was born on April 1, 1797, on a farm near Monkton, Vermont. Hiram, the first of twelve children born to Swift and Mary Chamberlain, was greatly influenced by his aunt Abigail, who taught him to read the Bible every day. He graduated from Andover Theological Seminary in Cambridge, Massachusetts, full of missionary zeal, and in 1825 he married Maria Morse, a schoolteacher he had known for five years. (She was a relative of Samuel Morse, inventor of the telegraph and Morse code.) Later he and Maria moved to Booneville, Missouri, where my great-grandmother Henrietta was born in 1835. Three years later, the Chamberlains moved to New Franklin, Missouri, where Maria died in childbirth. The following year,

The big house at Santa Gertrudis, which burned on January 4, 1912, and was replaced

Hiram married again, but in May 1840 his second wife died. He married Anna Griswold two years later, and they eventually had eight children.

Henrietta, close to her family, was sent, at about age fourteen, to finishing school at a minister's home in Holly Springs, Mississippi, east of Memphis. She was very homesick. Her father replied to her letters, telling her to be of good cheer and mindful of the needs of others, to read her Bible, and to work and study hard. He believed that faith, hope, and charity would sustain us all and that happiness was to be found in heaven. Henrietta was glad to rejoin her family on the houseboat in Brownsville, where in 1850, Hiram, the first Protestant minister on the Rio Grande, established the First Presbyterian Church.

FIRST PERMANENT SETTLER

In 1890 Grandfather Kleberg wrote, "Captain King was the first permanent settler between the Nueces River and the Rio Grande. The Indians were thick in that region in those days, and it took a man of nerve to hold his own."[1]

The depression in Brownsville and Matamoros in the aftermath of war and the gold rush led to banditry on both sides of the river, and yellow fever, malaria, and cholera were rampant. Hoping for a healthier life, Richard and Henrietta made the move to Santa Gertrudis in 1854. A *jacal*, a brush and mud structure, was their first home. One day when Henrietta was taking bread from her outdoor oven, she heard a sound from her daughter, Nettie. When she turned to rock the cradle, she saw a half-naked Indian holding a club over her baby, pointing with his other hand to his mouth. Stifling her impulse to scream, she smiled and handed him a loaf of bread. He disappeared as quickly as he had come. Henrietta Chamberlain's faith had sustained her.

STOCKING THE VAST PRAIRIE

When the Civil War began, King, Kenedy, Charles Stillman, and Francisco Yturria sided with their friend, Gen. Robert E. Lee. Besides the friendship they shared, all believed in states' rights, the same issue that drove Texas to secede from Mexico (Santa Anna was determined to run Mexico from Mexico City with no rights for the states). Santa Gertrudis became an important stopover for Confederate goods going to and from Brownsville. At the ranch, fresh horses and oxen were available, in addition to good water, meat, salt, and people who could make repairs. At the river, Kenedy saw to it that goods such as cotton were consigned to trusted Mexican citizens, primarily Stillman and Yturria. Unless the North wanted war with Mexico, once goods were consigned to Mexican citizens they could be shipped up- or downriver with impunity.

As the war intensified, bandits from Mexico, as well as Indians and renegades, raided the sparsely populated ranches. King left home in mid-December without telling anyone where he was going. If the Yankees came looking for him, no one would have to lie. He was trying to recover his herd of cattle from Mexican thieves while dodging Yankees, but the herd had crossed the river. King went into the thieves' camp, but, as they were in Mexico, he could not recover the cattle. Back at Santa Gertrudis, he found the place ransacked, with his wife and children gone. He learned that the Yankees had come shooting all the way to his house. When Francisco Alvarado, who was staying with the pregnant Mrs. King, ran to the door shouting, "Don't shoot! There are only women and children here," the troops fired, killing him right beside Henrietta.[2] She and her children departed for San Antonio to stay until the war was over. They stopped at San Patricio while Henrietta gave birth to her second son, Lee, named after the good friend who had recommended the site for the ranch home at Santa Gertrudis.

After the war, King continued to buy good ranch land, especially if it was near Santa Gertrudis or toward Brownsville. He stocked it with the best Longhorns he could find. He also improved his horses, buying a Kentucky stallion for more than he paid for his original ranch. He had wells and cisterns dug, put in earthen dams, built barbed-wire fences, and invested in the railroad from Corpus Christi to Laredo. Good lawyers in Brownsville and Corpus Christi worked on clearing titles to his lands. He recorded all he bought or sold in ledgers.

To stock the vast prairies of Santa Gertrudis, in a region then known as the Wild Horse Desert or Desert of the Dead (Desierto de los Muertos), King traveled to drought-stricken Cruillas, Mexico, where a rancher wished to sell his entire herd. A deal was struck. Then, seeing the sadness in the faces of the ranch folk, King asked the *hacendado* if he could invite them to journey with him to his ranch, where he had plenty of work. Many accepted and became *Kineños*, or King's men, a title they still value.

The Kineños built homes for themselves and a nice pine and cypress one-story house with a front porch for the Kings. The house soon became two stories for a growing family and visitors, mostly the Kings' friends, who had also started ranching. The Kenedys, Armstrongs, and Yturrias, as well as the Chamberlains, often stopped on their travels by horse-drawn coach between Brownsville and San Antonio.

In those days, when a herd was sold, the brand went with it. We don't know for sure whether the brand *la vivorita* (little snake)—now the running W—came with the herd from Cruillas or another in the same era.

UP THE TRAIL

Before the Civil War the only market for large numbers of cattle was for their hides and tallow, which was used to make soap, candles, and other goods.

Las Matanzas (the killings) is still the name of a pasture at Santa Gertrudis; it refers to the cattle slaughtering that took place there. Salt from the Sal del Rey, west of present-day Raymondville, was the only preservative besides ashes. There was no refrigeration. Transportation to ports was on two-wheeled ox carts, horseback, or foot to ships docked in Corpus Christi and Brownsville.

King's herds were among the first sent up the trails, and over the years he and others drove millions of Longhorns to the railheads in Kansas, where they were sold. There was great demand for beef in the increasingly populated cities of the East, as well as on Indian reservations and in mining fields in the West. The Longhorns were so hardy that they could actually gain weight walking and grazing their way to market. King's contracts with herd bosses ensured that the ranch bore relatively little of the risk. Once King's cattle were rounded up, branded, and readied to go up the trail, a herd boss signed a contract making him the owner of the cattle and the outfit that went with them, and further making him the employer of all hands, responsible for wages and provisions during the drive. King furnished him an account with the cash required for such expenses. The boss bought the herd by signing a note for both the value of the road outfit (horses, wagons, and other equipment) and for the cattle at their current price in Texas, payable to King upon sale of the herd to northern buyers. The partnership consisted in a split of the profits, which was the difference, after road expenses, between the price the herd boss paid King and the price he got for the cattle in Kansas.[3]

The June 14, 1884, *Texas Live Stock Journal* reported that "Capt. King has shipped 24,000 head of cattle, 10,000 of which were fours and upwards, and the balance ones, twos and threes. From what we could learn, there have been considerable losses on account of careless handling at Wichita Falls and beyond."[4] The

June 23, 1883, *Cuero Bulletin* tells how King protected some of his profits: "Six thousand head stampeded upon nearing the Nueces, on the drive from King's Rio Grande pastures, and it is said nearly half of them were lost. . . . The immense herds broke wildly for the river as soon as they realized they were nearing it, and many of them, being very weak, went down under the feet of the others. So far as we are able to learn, the loss will come upon Mr. Stevens, as we are told that in his arrangement with Capt. King, the risk of the drive rested upon Mr. Stevens."[5]

It was said that King sometimes had as many as three large herds on the trail at one time, each "shaped" according to color—paint horses, for example, were ridden by cowboys driving paint cattle. King would go to the railhead destination and, depending on price and volume, send messages to hurry or delay on the trail. All the cattle were branded with the running W or with Mrs. King's HK brand before leaving the ranch.

As the great trail drives commenced, the Texas livestock industry was born. Soon the railroads came. The country was fenced, and trail driving was history.

FAMILY

By the late 1800s, the Kings had money for travel, for enlarging the ranch house, and for educating their children. When the family lived at Santa Gertrudis, the five King children frequently traveled to other ranch homes, Texas cities, and Mexico. Later, trains carried them to Colorado, Missouri, and Kentucky to further their educations.

Nettie, the eldest, married a Yankee, Colonel Atwood. She was disinherited by her father but later reinstated by her mother. Richard was given La Puerta, a lovely ranch near Corpus Christi, when he married. Mrs. King thought this was a good solution, as young Richard liked farming while the Captain despised it. Ella

married, but I know almost nothing about her except that my father bought her inherited land from a descendant for King Ranch. Lee was his father's choice to take over ranch management, but he died young of pneumonia in St. Louis. Alice Gertrudis King, after schooling in St. Louis, stayed with her parents at Santa Gertrudis. Sometimes Henrietta sent her on trips with the Captain, as she thought Alice's presence would curb his drinking.

We will never know the full extent of my great-grandmother King's gifts. She was an intensely private and deeply religious woman whose gentle voice often proclaimed, "God loves you!" She gave money to Louis Pasteur for his rabies research and to build Spohn Hospital in honor of the family's beloved doctor. Later she gave land for schools and churches in Kingsville. She was kind and generous, never seeking personal recognition.

ALONG CAME KLEBERG...

One day in 1881, Richard King was opposed in court over a tresspass dispute by a young lawyer who argued so well that he defeated King. The lawyer, who was new in town, was trying his first case in Nueces County. Immediately after the adverse verdict, Captain King introduced himself to Robert Justus Kleberg II and invited him to Santa Gertrudis. On July 24, 1881, Robert wrote his parents of his visit to the ranch:

> We had a delightful trip out to his ranch—he drove a pair of fine fast horses and in two hours we were at his ranch—he had in his carriage plenty of ice, wine and cigars, so the heat

did not bother us much. . . . I stayed at his house from Monday until Saturday morning. In the evening we went riding—one day we were out all day. He showed me his pasture and cattle—he owns about 1,000,000 acres of land 137 leagues in one grant and most of it is fine land—and all of it stocked with cattle, horses, mules and sheep. Near the lakes where the cattle come to drink could be seen as many as 3,000 head at a time, but the country is very dry at present—no rains at all.[6]

At the end of the week the Captain sent young Kleberg back to the railroad depot with suitable wine and ice. Kleberg wrote, "He wants us to attend to his legal business."[7] He accepted a retainer of $5,000 a year to handle Captain King's legal affairs. On this visit, young Alice was fascinated by Robert Kleberg's red beard and was attracted to him.

Over the next five years King had considerable title work and other legal matters for Robert to address. Meanwhile, the Captain's legendary strength and energy were failing. He had led a hard life from his earliest years, and not even whiskey could lessen the pain that had developed in his abdomen. Robert asked permission to marry Alice Gertrudis, and King gave it. Then the Captain and Henrietta traveled to San Antonio to see whether doctors there could help him, but to no avail. King died at the Menger Hotel on April 14, 1885. The diagnosis was stomach cancer. He was buried in San Antonio, but later, after Henrietta's death, he was moved to Chamberlain Cemetery beside her.

On June 17, 1886, Robert Justus Kleberg and Alice Gertrudis King were married in the house at Santa Gertrudis. Mrs. King accompanied them on their honeymoon.

As for Kleberg family history, legend has it that the Klebergs descend from Charlemagne. Another tale, one that Mana used to tell, is that a young Kleberg went off to the wars, leaving behind his fiancée. Having heard nothing of him for some years, she entered a convent, intent on taking her vows. One day she was surprised by her beloved, who made his way into the convent hidden in a load of hay. He took her out as he had come in. A German king whose life young Kleberg saved had given him a ring, saying, "If you ever need anything, send a message with the ring so I will know it is from you." The ring went with a petition for a church wedding. Granted, of course.

(preceding page)
7 Robert J. Kleberg Sr. family, circa 1903. Back row from left: Henrietta, Robert J., Alice, Richard. Front row: Sarah, Bob Jr., Alice Gertrudis Kleberg (Mana).

8 Mrs. Richard King with great-grandchildren, circa 1910

(following pages)
9 Captain Richard King, circa 1885

10 Captain Richard King and his family, circa 1880

11 Henrietta Morse Chamberlain King, circa 1920

12 Alice Gertrudis King Kleberg (Mana)

10

12

Kleberg ingenuity

Robert Justus Kleberg, circa 1880

Robert Justus Kleberg was born on September 10, 1803, in Herstelle, Westfalia, Germany. In her 1928 diary, my grandmother, Alice Gertrudis King Kleberg, wrote a quote from Robert Justus Kleberg I, her father-in-law: "I wish to live under a republican form of government with unbounded personal religion and political liberty—free from the petty tyranny and the many ideologies and evils of the old countries. Prussia smarted at that time under an offensive military despotism. I was, and have ever remained, an enthusiastic lover of republican institutions and I expected to find in Texas, above all countries, the blessed land of my most fervent hopes."

As my grandmother tells the story in her diary, Robert received his law degree from the University of Göttingen. After serving in various judicial positions, he, like many others in Germany, "became dissatisfied with the military and administrative despotism prevalent everywhere" and immigrated to America. She adds that it must be taken for granted "that any grandson of the grand old pioneer, Robert Kleberg, now a nephew enthusiastic from Texas in the Congress at Washington, will remain steadfast in this faith, of unbounded personal religious and political liberty, the glory of American democracy." She was referring to Rudolph Kleberg. Later, her son Richard Mifflin Kleberg would serve in Congress.

In Germany, Great-grandfather Kleberg wished to marry Rosalie Von Roeder, a daughter of Anton Ludwig Von Roeder and Caroline Louise Sack. She accepted his proposal after exacting a promise that he take her to the New World. The senior Von Roeders waited in Germany with the bride and groom for the birth of Clara S. Kleberg, who arrived on November 29, 1833. In August 1834, they set sail from Bremen on their journey to join other family and friends in Texas.

Describing their arrival in Texas and their subsequent shipwreck, my great-grandfather Kleberg wrote, "About two weeks after we landed in New Orleans we sailed for Brazoria, Texas. After a voyage of eight days, we wrecked off of Galveston Island, on December 22, 1834. It is impossible to name with certainty the exact point of the island at which we were stranded but I think it was not far from the center, about ten miles above the present site of the city [Galveston] on the beach side. The island was a perfect wilderness, inhabited only by deer, wolves and rattlesnakes."[8]

He continued, "I heard for the first time of the whereabouts of my relatives, who had preceded us. Louis and Albrecht von Roeder had located about fourteen miles from San Felipe on a league and labor of land. We found them in a miserable hut and in a pitiful condition. They were emaciated by disease and want, and without money. Tears of joy streamed from their eyes when they beheld us."[9]

Later, Great-grandfather described the work required to start their new lives: "Not being accustomed to manual labor, we proceeded very slowly. We had supplied ourselves with everything necessary. We had all sorts of tools, household and kitchen furniture, and clothing, which we had brought with us from Germany." By September 1835 they had finished building two log houses, using planks from post oak trees to make the floor and ceiling, and had planted a field of ten acres in corn and cotton. "We now moved the members of our party who had remained at Harrisburg to our settlement with our wagons and teams."[10]

The community that resulted from this hard work was called Cat Spring, as someone had seen a bobcat drinking from the nearby spring. The town boasts the oldest agricultural society west of the Mississippi River.

TEXAS INDEPENDENCE

While the Klebergs, Von Roeders, and other families worked to organize their new lives, Santa Anna imprisoned Stephen F. Austin in Mexico City for daring to petition for Texas' statehood separate from Coahuila. Santa Anna, already irritated by the political dissent over whether Saltillo or Monclova was the capital of Coahuila, was determined to remove authority from the states in favor of a strong central government in Mexico City. At last Austin was released from prison, but incidental revolts were occurring in Texas. Certain that the United States was encouraging new colonists to reject Mexican rule, Santa Anna gathered a well-equipped army in 1835 for his march to "inspect Texas." He had decided to crush any insurrection—to take no prisoners and to get rid of colonists he had not personally authorized. There ensued the massacre of the defendants of the Alamo at San Antonio in March 1836. Shortly after, a murderous assault on Goliad (La Bahía) ended with all prisoners shot.

The Klebergs and Von Roeders were not the only colonists alarmed by these events. A rapid exodus, known as the "runaway scrape," of women and children toward Louisiana with hoped-for protection from the U.S. Army began. As soon as Robert Justus Kleberg could, he joined Company D, First Regiment of the Texas Volunteers. They soon joined Gen. Sam Houston near the junction of Buffalo Bayou and the San Jacinto River. On the afternoon of April 21, 1836, what could have been a devastating encounter with a superior number of soldiers ended quickly with the Texans' capture of Santa Anna. They were aided in this capture by the mulatto slave Emily Morgan, who sent word to the Texans when and where to find Santa Anna in her company. Colonel Morgan gave Emily her freedom for her brave sacrifice. This historic battle at San Jacinto resulted in Texas's independence from Mexico. Knowing Judge Kleberg's courage and integrity, Houston appointed him one of three guards to see that Santa Anna neither escaped nor was murdered.[11] Robert Kleberg I then helped escort the Mexican army to Mexico, stopping on the way to bury the Texas dead at Goliad.

REPUBLIC OF TEXAS

Having no money, the state of Texas rewarded Kleberg for his service with a gift of 350 acres. Several years later, Sam Houston, then president of Texas, appointed Kleberg president of land commissions. President Lamar appointed him chief justice of Austin County. In October 1845, he was granted 4,000 acres located thirteen miles southeast of Dallas. Today a few buildings in the town named Kleberg remain.

By the late 1840s Kleberg had moved his family to DeWitt County, where he built one of the county's first schools. His public service included terms as county commissioner and chief justice. When the Civil War broke out in 1861, he organized a company to fight for the Confederacy; particularly important to him was the republican form of government and states' rights. At age sixty, he was not accepted for active service.

In John Henry Brown's *The Indian Wars and Pioneers of Texas*, my great-grandfather is remembered as "a man of deep and most varied learning. Besides knowledge of Greek and Latin, he controlled three modern languages and read their literatures in the originals. A man of urbane manners and courtly address, his intercourse with men, whether high or low, educated or ignorant, was ever characterized by a plain and noble dignity, free of assumption or vanity."[12]

Robert Justus Kleberg died in 1888 at the age of eighty-six and was buried in the Eckhardt family cemetery near Yorktown. (His daughter Clara had married an Eckhardt.) A headstone, in the form of a tent, is engraved with "Remember the Alamo." Together, Robert and Rosalie had raised four sons and four daughters. The family held faith, integrity, service, and education in high regard and earned respect at all levels of society.

Robert J. Kleberg Sr.

Kleberg family, circa 1903. Clockwise from upper left: Mary, Alice, Henrietta, Minerva, Richard King Jr., Sarah, Henrietta Chamberlain King, and Bob

Infant Bob Kleberg Jr. with his mother, Alice King Kleberg (Mana), circa 1898

Thanksgiving 1943. Back row from left: Bob Kleberg Jr., Katherine Kleberg, Mary Lewis Kleberg, Richard Kleberg Jr. Front row: Etta Larkin, Mana, B. K. Johnson

NEXT GENERATION

Little is known of Robert and Rosalie's oldest son, Otto, but Rudolph and Marcellus left deep tracks in Texas history. Rudolph, who was born in a log cabin at Cat Spring, studied law in San Antonio and entered the Texas bar in 1872. He was DeWitt County attorney and was later elected to the Texas senate. In 1896 he was elected to the U.S. House of Representatives, with his son, Caesar, joining him in Washington as his assistant. Rudolph was known for his benevolence and knowledge.

Marcellus graduated from Washington and Lee University School of Law in 1872 and was elected to the 13th Texas Legislature. He married in 1875 and established a law practice in Galveston, where he served as city attorney and commissioner. He was a charter member of the Texas Bar Association and a regent of the University of Texas.

My grandfather, Robert Justus Kleberg, was born December 5, 1853, on the family farm near Meyersville, Texas. Like his father, he studied law, attending the University of Virginia and returning to Texas. He became a partner in the Stayton Kleberg law firm, practicing in Corpus Christi.

IMPROVING THE STOCK

Robert Justus Kleberg and Alice Gertrudis King had five children, Richard Mifflin, Henrietta Rosa, Alice King, Robert Justus Jr. (my father), and Sarah Spohn.

Henrietta King inherited all of Captain King's property and his debts. She asked Grandfather Kleberg to manage her vast estate. A few years later, in September 1890, he stated: "We have between 680,000 and 700,000 acres altogether lying in Nueces and Webb counties, and I don't know exactly how many cattle, but 100,000 head would not be far out of the way. We don't drive any of our cattle overland now, but sell to parties who ship from the ranch by rail. Since the boom of 1882 the bottom has dropped out of the cattle business, but there is a somewhat better demand of late, and I look for upward prices ere long."[13]

The need to drive cattle long distances had dried up. Cattle were now shipped in rail cars to markets in Kansas City, St. Louis, Chicago, and Fort Worth. Texas ranchers began to focus on improving their stock, with the goal of producing more meat in less time with the same natural resources, water and grass. No longer needed, the Longhorn, whose principle value was its ability to walk the trail, was replaced by Herefords and Shorthorns, which ranchers brought to the region to improve the livestock's meat value.

To improve and replace Captain King's great herds of Longhorns, Robert Kleberg II kept only the highest-grade bulls on the ranch and exercised great care in breeding. The best bulls were bred to their higher-grade cows, and there was no inbreeding. Grandfather created an innovative system of marketing King Ranch cattle. The August 4, 1897, *Texas Stock and Farm Journal* reported: "A buyer who this past spring purchased the yearlings from the [Kleberg] herd was so pleased with his bargain that he has now contracted for the yearlings of 1898 and 1899 and paid money down on both contracts. Contracting for cattle one and two years before they are born is a new one for Texas Cattlemen."[14] Grandfather also experimented with raising corn, milo, cotton, potatoes, and onions. He planted date, palm, fig, olive, and citrus trees.

KINGSVILLE

Kingsville was founded in 1904. Soon hundreds arrived seeking jobs, homes, churches, schools—all the things a town could offer. On July 4, 1904, the St. Louis, Brownsville & Mexico Railway reached Kingsville. My father told me he rode in the cab of the first train in 1903, arriving at the new town site. I don't know whether his siblings were with him, but later Daddy, along with his brother and sisters, rode the train to Corpus Christi to school. There they stayed with their grandmother King in her Victorian house. She believed traveling was educational, so she often took the whole family to Colorado, St. Louis, and other places.

CATTLE RAISERS ASSOCIATION

The Cattle Raisers Association of Texas was created in 1877 to protect its members' livestock from thieves. In 1899 and 1900, Grandfather was elected president of this organization, which later became the Texas and Southwestern Cattle Raisers Association. In December 1916, cattlemen meeting in Corpus Christi were invited to tour King Ranch. Association minutes reported that "after coffee, we were conducted across the most fertile looking country in the world to the town of Kingsville. . . . The remainder of the afternoon was spent looking at the model dairy and farms and driving over several pastures where thousands of beef cattle grazed contentedly. And, notwithstanding the drought that was not broken until July, the purebred Shorthorns and Herefords looked well, many being fat."[15]

ADIOS AMIGO MIO

During his later years, Grandfather Kleberg was in poor health; Grandmother Kleberg, whom we called Mana, loved to take him for drives around the ranch. She thought he enjoyed my company and that of my cousin B. K. Johnson, so she put us in the backseat with her. To keep us quiet, Mana fed us lots of crackers and told us to sit still and not make any noise. As Grandfather's condition grew worse, his children were called home. When he died on October 10, 1932, at the age of seventy-eight, all except his daughter, Henrietta Larkin, who was living in New York, were present.

Grandfather's efforts contributed immeasurably to the improvement of the land and livestock originally operated by Captain King. His dedicated leadership helped stimulate the development of Kingsville, the surrounding areas, and the state. The *Kingsville Record* eulogized him thus: "Of all the eloquent and sincere tributes paid the great South Texan, none touched the hearts more than the farewell of a grizzled old Mexican of the range, who came to gaze for the last time on the face of his good friend. With tear-dimmed eyes and trembling lips, he looked long and tenderly on the silent face before him, and before turning to go, half sobbingly said, 'Adios, amigo mio.' "[16]

His funeral was one of the largest in Texas history, causing his Masonic graveside ceremonies to be delayed for several hours. Justus was a fitting middle name for Grandfather, who frequently asserted, "Those who possess power, property, or influence must hold it in trust for the use of their fellow man."

MANA

My grandmother, Mana, was physically petite and, as I recall, always dressed in black or gray. She was constantly mourning the death of a family member, from her father, Captain King, to her daughter, Sarah. She was a natural-born worrier, and every night before lights-out she went around making sure that the women, children, married couples, and their families staying upstairs in the big house were in bed and comfortable. She did not check downstairs, because that was reserved for single men and men traveling alone.

On one occasion, Daddy and the men were working cattle at the Laureles division. They had camped for the night when a strong norther hit. Around 2:00 A.M., he awoke to the sounds of a caravan arriving in camp. Mana had sent out blankets and a bed for his comfort. When he realized this, he was outraged and sent them back. He said that since the other men didn't have these luxuries, he didn't need them either.

B. K. Johnson and I noticed that Mana always put others before herself. I recall a man who worked in the big house; every day he would ask her for ten dollars, and without hesitation she gave it to him. We thought she was becoming forgetful in her old age and that he was taking advantage of her. In retrospect, I think she probably felt his needs were greater than her own.

Shortly after Mana's death on July 31, 1944, the *Corpus Christi Caller* wrote: "Mrs. Kleberg was described by friends who knew her best as a woman of strong mind and character, but with gentleness of spirit and complete unselfishness. The hospitality of the King Ranch, under her direction, was traditional and no one in need was ever turned away empty-handed. The coffee pot was always on."[17]

(following pages)
13 Robert J. Kleberg Sr. and Bob Kleberg Jr. at the reins, circa 1898

14 Robert J. Kleberg Sr. with Alice Kleberg

15 From left: Richard Kleberg, Robert J. Kleberg Sr., Bob Kleberg Jr., circa 1907

16 From left: Mana, Robert J. Kleberg Sr., Richard Kleberg, Caesar Kleberg, Bob Kleberg Jr., Tom Armstrong

13

16

Young Bob, a close observer

My father, Robert J. Kleberg Jr., was born on March 29, 1896, in Corpus Christi. His early education began on the ranch, where he worked with his father, his cousin Caesar Kleberg, and the Kineños.

My father and his brother, Richard, who was nine years older, often rode in the automobile Uncle Dick had received from Mrs. King when he graduated from high school. In those days there were few roads, so they drove over fields and pastures. One day, Daddy crank-started the car as he had done so often before. The crank hurled out of control, striking his right arm. The force broke his arm and knocked him to the ground. Uncle Dick set Daddy's arm with a makeshift splint. When they got back to the house, Mana and Grandfather Kleberg insisted that Daddy go to a doctor, who reset his arm. After this, Daddy could not rotate his arm properly; though he could use it for most tasks, he was hampered when roping. He was always sure Dick had set it right the first time.

Daddy had grown up in a place where days began at 4:00 A.M. Whether he was on horseback or on the ground, he worked with the Kineños, many of whose forefathers had come to Texas from Mexico to work for Captain King. By the time Daddy was grown, he and the other cowboys were roping, dipping, branding, dehorning, castrating, and vaccinating thousands of calves annually. At his father's side, he learned to see

Bob Kleberg Jr., circa 1904

quality in an animal by examining bone structure and the "look in the eye"; the shape of the head was a guide to the shape of the body.

Though he learned much from the men around him, there was always more to master. Leroy Denman Jr., former King Ranch president and legal adviser, recalls: "When he was a boy, his grandmother King and his father insisted that he go every night to the old Casa Ricardo Hotel to listen to Judge Wells. After supper, the judge would tell him about land titles, history, and legal problems. Bob was very tired. He had been up before daybreak and had worked all day. As the judge continued, Bob became so sleepy he could hardly hold his eyes open. That's when Judge Wells shook his finger at him and said, 'Young man, the Lord gave you a mind and he expects you to use it!' "

TAKING CARE OF THE LAND

My father was close to Grandfather Kleberg. Once Daddy told me about the time he sold some steers as a young fellow. He was proud of the deal and told his father, "I got the very top dollar for this bunch of steers!" His father said, "Bob, you shouldn't have done that." My father didn't understand. He thought he had done a great job.

Grandfather continued, "You've got to leave the other man room to make a little money. If you don't, he won't be able to buy any more of your cattle. Always try to be able to have made a profit, but leave the other man room to make a profit also. Don't try to get the very last dollar! The man will lose money and won't be back."

My father was proud of his ranching heritage and the experiences he had as a young man. Before he married my mother, he and his first cousin, Caesar Kleberg, had adjacent rooms in the big house. Caesar became his mentor and taught him about livestock, land, wildlife, and people. Daddy learned the importance of being a good steward of the land. He became an excellent shot and loved to hunt, but his love for wildlife made him back Caesar's efforts to establish seasons and bag limits at the state and federal levels.

PERPETUAL MOTION

Daddy graduated from Corpus Christi High School in 1914. His yearbook captions announced, "Robert Kleberg Senior Class Goat, Behold! The nearest thing to perpetual motion yet discovered. Can easily talk half a day and never think of stopping." When the yearbook staff asked what he admired most in a man, he responded, "Honesty." When asked what he admired most in a woman, he declared, "Modesty." He left the "future occupation" field blank, possibly revealing the uncertainty of his college plans. For graduation his grandmother King gave him a Stutz Bearcat.

UNIVERSITY OF WISCONSIN

While Bob was housebound with his broken arm, his father was persuasive about a plan to further his education.

Grandfather Kleberg had been the first to bring Jersey cattle to South Texas to start a dairy. He was also responsible for managing and upgrading thousands of cattle on Mrs. King's ranch with champion Hereford and Shorthorn bulls. He hoped Daddy would continue to make advancements in these areas and wanted him to study animal husbandry at the University of Wisconsin, which he believed offered the best course of study for that subject. Grandfather also knew Daddy wanted to study electrical engineering, so he made a proposal: "I'd like you to take animal husbandry, but if after two years you want to study electrical engineering, it's all right with me."

Daddy left for school in September 1914 and moved into his quarters at 630 Lake Street in Madison. His classes included agronomy, animal husbandry, agricultural economics, agricultural bacteria, agricultural engineering, chemistry, dairy husbandry, soils, agricultural chemistry, veterinary science, English, horticulture, physical education, gym, and military drill. Daddy's love of the land and livestock was obvious, as his highest grades were in agricultural courses.

Years later, my father recalled, "I studied genetics and not much of anything else. I also did a lot of studying on my own, just reading, which I have done ever since." My mother said the only book she knew he had read at the university was Alvin Sanders' *History of the Shorthorn Breed.* Though my father read many magazines and books about science, Sanders' book, with his theories on line breeding, inbreeding, and the need for a "prepotent" individual with desirable characteristics, influenced Daddy the most. In his own work with cattle and horse breeds, Daddy was a close observer and always applied scientific methods based on clear criteria.

Wisconsin winters were cold. When Daddy wasn't studying he enjoyed ice sailing, ice fishing, and snow shoeing. His outgoing nature led him to make new friends and generally enhance his social life by joining the Alpha Lambda chapter of the Sigma Chi fraternity. He made many friends there, including two who shared his keen interest in breeding and genetics. Their companionship would stretch far beyond the University of

Bob Kleberg Jr. leaving to attend the University of Wisconsin, 1915

Wisconsin. Howard Rouse would one day help Daddy establish King Ranch in Kentucky, and Herbert Shipman was credited with bringing the first Santa Gertrudis cattle to Hawaii in 1951, when he bought two King Ranch bulls.

EARLY SEARCH FOR OIL

While my father was attending the University of Wisconsin, two wildcatters made an agreement with Grandfather Kleberg to search for oil on King Ranch. Their lease provided that drilling must be carried on continuously, and that every time a new well was started, one-quarter of the surrounding acreage had to be conveyed back to my grandfather, who was then free to sell it to competitors. Wallace Pratt, a Humble Oil representative, recalled, "On one of my visits to Kingsville, I brought up the Guffey and Galey lease with Mr. Kleberg Sr., but he told me he wanted his son, Robert Kleberg Jr., who would come home shortly from Wisconsin University, to take over part of the administration of the ranch, and to handle all business related to oil leases."[18]

In the late fall of 1916, Grandfather Kleberg had a stroke. Daddy returned home, ending his formal education. For the rest of his life he continued to read and seek out individuals who knew more than he did, making the world his classroom.

On September 26, 1933, Humble leased the lands to be partitioned among Mana's heirs—about 971,700 acres—along with the Santa Gertrudis headquarters tract and additional acreages. Oil and gas were found on the estate's land in May 1939, almost six years after the lease was signed.[19]

18

19

22

23

25

Campbells

Scotland to Canada, to Kansas, citizenship, to
Congress, and life in the U.S. capital

From humble beginnings

SCOTLAND TO NOVA SCOTIA

About 1820, my mother's great-grandparents, Alexander Colin Campbell and his wife, Janet Urquhart, left Argyleshire in Scotland on the *John Walker*, eventually landing on the craggy coast of Cape Breton Island, off Nova Scotia, at Sydney Mines. The means of livelihood there included mining, small farming, and deep sea fishing. The Campbells spoke Gaelic, read the Bible, and worked hard. They had seven children: Isabella, Mary, Anna, Hannah, Donald, John, and a second Donald, called Daniel, my mother's grandfather. Did the first Donald die young? We don't know.

My great-grandfather, Daniel Campbell, was born in 1831 in Nova Scotia. In 1859, he married Mary McRae of Inverness, Scotland; she was adamant that they move far from the treacherous sea that claimed so many young men. They began to dream of the American West. After his father's death in 1866 and the end of the Civil War, Daniel and Mary and their children Murdoch, seven; Philip, five; Alexander, three; and Mary, two; and the widowed Janet set sail for Boston. Daniel bought a covered wagon, which he outfitted for the journey west. The family stopped in Argonia, Illinois, where Hannah Campbell was born on June 9, 1867.

WESTWARD HO

The entries in Grandfather Philip Campbell's journal begin there. We don't know whether his grandmother or mother helped him with it. Early entries show what life was like for the family:

June 1867. Father is making a wagon to move to Kansas.

July 7. All the family is getting in the wagon to start for Kansas. There is a crate of chickens fastened to the rear end of the wagon and a cow tied behind that. There is a plow fastened on one side of the wagon and some stovepipe on the other side. Everything else is in the wagon.

July 15. Mississippi River up; cannot get to the bridge for two days—went swimming and my back is burned to a blister.

July 22. Stopped in Missouri where Father is helping a farmer make hay.

August 7. About 4:00 in the afternoon, we stopped in the middle of a prairie where the grass is as high as the horses' back and everybody got out of the wagon. Father walked around and looked for the stones that marked the corners of the land. We slept in the wagon that night.

After traveling hundreds of miles, the family arrived at their destination, Flat Rock Valley in southeast Kansas' Neosho County. The 160-acre farm Daniel would eventually purchase was five miles from good water and nine miles from the Osage mission. No trees or even a wagon track could be seen. The bluestem grass was reminiscent of the sea they had left behind.

Daniel set the wagon bed and cover off the running gear so that his family would have shelter. Philip wrote, "While Father has gone to get lumber, three Indians came down through the grass where the wagon had made a trail. Mother put all the children in the wagon and got in herself. She then took a large butcher knife and hid it behind her and sat still in the wagon

Philip Pitt Campbell

until the Indians stuck their heads in the front end of the cover. One of them pointed to a piece of bacon that was tied to the cover of the wagon over Mother's head and made a motion to his mouth. Mother cut the string to the bacon and handed it to the Indian. They turned around and went away." Daniel soon built their home, which was "14 feet one-way and 16 feet on the other and about 8 feet high. Made of cottonwood boards standing up, a sod floor and several openings for windows covered with cloth."

More of Philip's journal entries:

April 15, 1867. While Father was away on a trip to the sawmill, a man with extraordinary intelligent features wearing the garb of a Catholic Priest rode up on a white pony. He was Father Schoenmaker of the Osage Mission. My mother had been brought up Presbyterian and had been taught that Catholics were far more dangerous than the bears in the woods. From the day of Father Schoenmaker's visit, she knew that her early instruction, with respect to the dangers of meeting a Catholic, were wrong.

December 24, 1867. Father went to the Mission. My Christmas present was a red, white and blue marble.

KANSAS SOD FARM

As the winter winds died down and the snow thawed, the countryside filled with millions of wildflowers. A new season had arrived, and it was time to go to the field. Philip Pitt wrote, "April 15, 1868. Father started to break prairie. My brother cut holes in the sod that had been turned over by the plow with an ax and I put the corn in the holes and tramped on it to cover it up." Daniel Campbell and his young sons continually worked the soil, preparing to plant buckwheat, oats, wheat, corn, sorghum, and beans.

On June 3, 1868, Daniel went to the district court in Erie, Kansas, where he "swore upon his oath and declared it was his bona-fide intention to become a citizen of the United States of North America, and to renounce and abjure forever all allegiance and fidelity to every foreign power, prince, potentate state and sovereignty, and particularly to Queen Victoria of the Kingdom of Great Britain."[20]

In addition to his small grain crops, Daniel earned money using his horses and wagons. When possible, he hauled lumber, dry goods, and other freight for local merchants. No matter how hard he worked, though, times were hard. During the blustery winter of 1870, my great-grandfather butchered two hogs he had fed for months; he hoped to trade the meat for shoes and other goods. He was disappointed when he got to town: "The storekeeper said he had all the meat he needed and would not trade shoes for more meat. Father brought the meat back home." On December 10, Philip Pitt wrote, "Father took a load of corn to town to trade for shoes. The storekeeper said he had all the corn he needed. He had to bring the corn back." On December 20, Philip still had no shoes: "Father said the reason was the train was coming to the Mission soon and everybody he once hauled freight for was waiting on the railroad."

Though Daniel's hands were callused from years of hard labor and his face was leathered from the blistering sun and wind, he never deserted his dream of helping his children get a proper education. In the spring of 1873, he announced, "I saw the red-winged blackbirds at the creek."[21] This was a good sign, and Great-grandfather Campbell felt optimistic about the coming year. He gave an acre of land for a new schoolhouse and lodging to the man who built it. It was in this one-room school that my mother's father (Philip Pitt), her uncle Murdoch, and her aunt Mary started school.

Then matters took a turn for the worse. Daniel suddenly fell ill, dying on February 20, 1873, at the age of forty-seven. He left a widow, four young sons, and two daughters. Philip wrote, "The Baptist preacher,

Congressman Philip Pitt
Campbell, late 1930s

Jonas Johnston, and all the neighbors came to our house. The preacher preached the funeral sermon. Then they put the coffin in Mr. Holly's wagon and went to the graveyard about 7 miles away. Mother did not go with us." Daniel Campbell is buried in Fowler Cemetery in Walnut, six and a half miles east of Erie.

Daniel's determination, faith in God, and hope for the future were not enough to overcome the hardships of his life on the land. His widow, Mary McCrae, prematurely gave birth to a baby girl, Dolena, just a few days after his funeral. No more is heard of that child. Mary had work to do to raise her children and keep her land from being seized by carpetbaggers.

TWO BROTHERS

Philip and Murdoch inherited the tremendous burden of operating the farm. They were doing men's work at ages ten and twelve. They began by plowing. On March 25, 1873, Philip wrote: "Murdoch and I put some wheat in sacks and went to the mill. We took the sacks to the back-end of the wagon, and with the end-gate out, we used boards for a slide to slide the sacks on to the wagon. We went to the mill and stayed until our grinding was done. We did not get back until way after dark." Mr. Holly helped them thresh wheat with his new machine after the boys had cut and dried it. They made 325 bushels. In September, they planted wheat and in October put up hay. They took corn to town on December 20 and got something for Christmas. In January 1874 they took turns going to school, but March had them plowing for oats, followed by corn planting.

The two continued to work together in the fields and took care of the family. It wasn't long, however, before Murdoch began spending more time pursuing his education—grade school, high school, and finally Baker College, where he studied to be a Methodist minister.

YOUNG LOVE

On June 20, 1879, at the age of seventeen, Philip Pitt wrote:

I went to Lawyer Stillwell's office and told him I was tired of working as a hired hand on the farm and would like to take care of his horse and cow for my board and study law in his office. He looked at my bare feet and my old straw hat with a hole in the top of it, that I was holding, and asked me how much I had been to school. I told him very little; that I had not been to school for the last two years. Then he said I should go to school and study a lot of other things before I started studying law. I thanked him and he got up and went to the door with me when I went out.

As a young man, Philip Pitt became fond of the pastor's daughter, Clara Anderson. He was often invited to dinner at the Andersons' home after church. There he and Clara would talk about *Romeo and Juliet* and other Shakespeare stories. When she went away to school, Philip wrote her often but never received a reply.

In November 1880, he learned from a mutual friend of his and Clara's "that she was embarrassed and afraid her friends would see my writing with my awful punctuation and capitals." He was more determined than ever to teach himself to read: "January 10, 1881. I got through reading Paul's Epistles to the Romans today. Have read Matthew, Mark, Luke and John this winter." In September 1882, Philip met with Dr. William Henry Sweet, president of Baker University, to see if he might start school in the lowest class. When the president asked about his education, Philip said that he had "probably spent three months all told in a country school; that I never got farther than fractions in arithmetic and I had not studied grammar." When Dr. Sweet asked what he had read, "I told him principally the Bible and Shakespeare. He told me there was no better reading than that." Philip, now twenty, began his studies in Mrs. Baker's class in the basement. The young boys and girls in her arithmetic class ranged in age from seven to twelve. She gave them lessons for the next day and invited those who wished to study grammar to stay. Six little girls and Philip volunteered.

During his time at Baker University he evolved from a barefoot boy into a handsome, dynamic young man with an attractive personality. Fond of Shakespeare early in life, he also came to love the poems of Robert Burns and other writers.

A RESONANT VOICE

Philip Pitt Campbell enjoyed debating, and in 1887 he competed in a statewide contest. "I sat in the audience when he won the state oratorical contest. What a handsome fellow he was! What a noble, resonant voice! What a commanding presence," remarked a Mr. Guyer of Kansas City.[22] Grandfather Campbell earned the opportunity to represent Kansas in the nationwide debate at Bloomington, Illinois, on May 5. There he walked onto the stage and declared his passion for freedom in "What of the Republic," part of which follows::

> Among the most passionate longings of the human beast are longings for liberty. The centuries have seen the fondest hopes of a liberty-loving people realized. They have also seen all that pertains to liberty crushed, except hope.

> During the centuries of darkness, bloodshed and barbarism that followed the downfall of the ancient republics, the seeds of liberty were again germinating throughout continental Europe. Growth and maturity, however, were impossible in a land surrounded by tyranny and overshadowed by despotism.

> In order that a people may cultivate the principles of civil and religious liberty, they must have a land geographically and physically peculiar to their purpose, and as varied as its natural resources are the proclivities of its inhabitants.

Such a land is North America, and upon the shores of New England, the pilgrims planted in the light of learning and Christianity, the tree of liberty under whose branches thirteen fair sisters sat and sang the songs of freedom and today, surrounded by the same halo, sitting beneath the branches of the same tree, thirty-eight American sisters are united in singing: "My country tis of thee, sweet land of liberty, of thee I sing."

Grandfather took second place that day to John H. Finley, who later became editor of the *New York Times*. He was also elected president of the National Oratorical Association and the following spring was designated valedictorian of Baker University. In the summer of 1888, at the age of twenty-five, he began studying law. He recalled, "When I was ready to read law in earnest, Judge Stillwell put me through a course of reading that prepared me for the examination for admission to the bar and I was admitted to practice by the judge himself."

In April 1889, Philip and his mother went to see Murdoch at Baldwin. Murdoch died the next day of bronchial pneumonia. Philip wrote in his journal, "His death shakes my faith. He had a wonderful ability and would have made a great preacher, if the Lord wants that kind of man to work for Him."

HELEN MARY GOFF

In June 1884, while Grandfather was visiting in Walnut, the bank president, Maj. James Goff, asked him to make a speech at a Fourth of July program he was arranging. Grandfather accepted, of course. After the event, he wrote in his diary, "I saw among others in the crowd a black-eyed girl whom I met. She is Major Goff's daughter. She was among those who spoke to me in a complimentary way about the speech."

About three years later, on June 17, 1887, Grandfather wrote, "I went down to Tisdale's yesterday afternoon and stayed until after supper. Helen Goff was there. I like her very much. She has been in Mt. Carroll,

Helen Goff Campbell (Granny), circa 1873

Illinois, at school for the last year." Helen graduated from Mt. Carroll Seminary in 1889, spent some time in Antwerp, New York, and returned to Walnut, where Philip was able to be with her more. They were married on November 23, 1892. Grandfather's bride, whom we called Granny, would have a powerful influence on him and those of us who came to know and love her.

Her parents were James Marcellus Goff and Mary F. Thomas. She had a brother, George, and a sister, Florence. Marcellus, her father, was born on December 24, 1840, in New York. When he was two his family moved to Wisconsin. He joined the Army of the Potomac in 1862. On September 20, 1863, at the close of the battle of Chickamauga in Georgia, he and other members of the 10th Wisconsin Infantry were forced to surrender to the Confederates. He said he had never felt so ashamed. Then he was afraid he would starve in Libby Prison at Richmond. When the war ended, Great-grandfather Goff moved to Kansas. Along with T. T. Percy, a friend, he bought about eighty acres and started the town of Walnut. Major Goff served as county school director, mayor, postmaster, and bank president. He promoted Decoration Day to honor Northern and Southern veterans who died in the war. He was also a Freemason. His wife, Mary Thomas, the daughter of Solomon Thomas and Mary Stowell, was from Wisconsin.

Philip Pitt and Helen Campbell lived in a large, two-story, wood-frame house at 1903 North Elm Street, in Pittsburg, Kansas. There they had four children. Dorothy was born in 1894; Colin, in 1895; and Elizabeth, in 1899. Helen Mary, my mother, was born in 1902.

Congressman Philip Pitt Campbell hunting on King Ranch, 1930s

OFF TO CONGRESS

On March 15, 1902, Grandfather was addressing an assembly in Pittsburgh when J. A. Nutman, president of the Manufacturers National Bank, entered the hall and announced, "We want you, Philip Campbell, as our candidate for Congress this year! Caucus will be held in this city and in Girard tonight, and it will be announced in the press tomorrow that you are Crawford County's candidate. You can't avoid it!"[23] Grandfather was elected to the 3rd U.S. Congressional District of Kansas that November, joining the 58th U.S. Congress.

Philip was at first discouraged because he saw the Democrats vote one way and Republicans vote the other, but soon he was actively fighting for the independent oil producers of Kansas against the monopoly of Standard Oil and its control of railroad freight rates. He said, "These monopolies are as merciless to the railroads as they are to their competitors, and their injustice in this is at last visited upon the public. Mr. Chairman, the great problem of today is the protection of individual rights—the socialism that would make atoms of us all is to be resisted whether it is socialism of the theorist or the monopolist."[24] Grandfather also worked for rural mail delivery and women's suffrage and spoke about Koch's discovery of the T.B. bacillus.

WINDSOR

In 1912 Grandfather purchased "Windsor" at 1240 South Arlington Ridge Road, in Arlington, Virginia. The main house and adjacent slave quarters, as well as a large barn, were on about ten acres at the top of the ridge. Below, on the Potomac River side, on flat brick-clay soil covered with trees, was another forty acres. The place had not recovered from its use as a hospital during the Civil War. It is believed to have belonged to the Custus branch of the George Washington family and then to the Lees before they built Arlington. I don't know whether the Lees spent any time at Arlington, about three miles northwest, as the property was already being used during the War Between the States as the National Cemetery. The view of the river and the capital nine miles away was spectacular, but the Campbell girls were afraid none of their boyfriends would travel so far to see them. Grandfather had the houses repaired and settled his family there, except for Colin, who had entered the U.S. Naval Academy. Granny did the landscaping and gardening, mostly before breakfast!

In August 1912, Grandfather went home to Kansas to see his mother, who was ill. She died in her home, at the age of eighty-seven, on August 28. Her children John, Philip Pitt, Mrs. Mary Munn of Pittsburg, Alex Campbell, and Mrs. R. J. Harlin (Aunt Hannah) of Erie were there. A Methodist minister conducted the funeral services. She was buried beside her husband and eldest son in Bethel Cemetery near Erie. She met the hardships of the early days with undaunted spirit, helped her boys farm, and made sure all were educated. In her later years, she and Alex lived with Hannah in Erie.

AFTER CONGRESS
In the fall of 1922, Grandfather was not re-elected to Congress, where he had served for twenty years. Later he explained, "My defeat was due to labor being idle and against me and they went to the polls, while my strongest support, being agriculture, were busy in the fields and couldn't make it to the polls."[25] Before completing his congressional duties, he assumed a key leadership position when the Speaker of the House became ill. He assumed the speakership on February 27, holding it until the session ended on March 4.

Grandfather continued to live at Windsor and opened a law office in Washington. He was selected to serve as parliamentarian of the Republican National Convention in 1924, held in Cleveland, Ohio. He was

counsel to Standard Oil Company of New Jersey, the Consolidated Oil Company of New York, and the Eagle Picher Lead Company of Joplin, Missouri. He also served as a director of the Fidelity Storage Company, belonged to the National Press Club and the Kappa Sigma Pi fraternity, and was a charter member of the Army-Navy Country Club.

LOCUST HILL FARM
In the spring of 1932, Grandfather purchased a lovely farm near Leesburg, Virginia. It consisted of about 400 acres of lush, grass-covered valleys, rolling hills, timber, streams, an old brick residence, farmhouses, and barns. At the time of purchase, the brick farmhouse had pigs in the cellar, sheep on the ground floor, and chickens upstairs. Grandfather spent years fixing it up, with Granny's help and encouragement. It was rumored that Lafayette had fought a duel on the lawn. Grandfather loved to ride over the fields inspecting the crops he and the farm manager had agreed to plant. He would round up grandchildren to work on the stone road or build a dam with stones and logs, so we could swim in the stream. He told us what to do, but how to do it was left to us. There were sows with piglets, cows and calves, a few sheep, horses, and a borrowed pony whose favorite trick was to run to the barn, throwing us grandkids on the way.

In early 1941, my parents went to Washington to be with Grandfather, who had become ill. The diagnosis was blood congestion in his brain. Philip Pitt Campbell died on May 26, 1941. W. W. Graves paid him the following compliment: "He might have been a strong contender for the presidency had he not been born on foreign soil, Nova Scotia, which made him ineligible."[26]

When I think about Grandfather, I remember him wearing stocks or high-button collars. He seemed a little austere; he was very kind and loving, though not given to hugging and kissing or gifts to show it. I remember Granny and Grandfather visiting at Santa Gertrudis and in camp at Norias. They always came to Texas on the train and would stay for a few happy days.

(preceding pages)
25 Helen Goff Campbell (Granny) and children. Clockwise from upper right: Elizabeth, Dorothy, Helen, and Colin, circa 1904.

(following pages)
26 Campbell home on the Kansas prairie, Philip Pitt Campbell framed by the doorway, circa 1870

27 Philip Pitt Campbell, circa 1870

28 Congressman Philip Pitt Campbell in Washington, D.C., circa 1910

29 Helen Goff Campbell (Granny) in Washington, D.C., circa 1910

30 Congressman Philip Pitt Campbell with President Warren G. Harding in Washington, D.C.

31 Helen Goff Campbell, circa 1894

32 Congressman Philip Pitt Campbell (right) with (from left) Tom Armstrong, Nelson Rockefeller, others unknown at King Ranch, late 1930s

33 From left: Alice King Kleberg (Mana), Bob Kleberg Jr., Helen C. Kleberg, Helen Goff Campbell (Granny), Congressman Philip Pitt Campbell, 1930s

34 Helen Goff Campbell (Granny) in the kitchen, 1950s

35 Congressman Philip Pitt Campbell at Los Amigos Camp, 1930s

26

27

THE PORTRAIT Gallery
Zimmerman
SAINT PAUL.

31

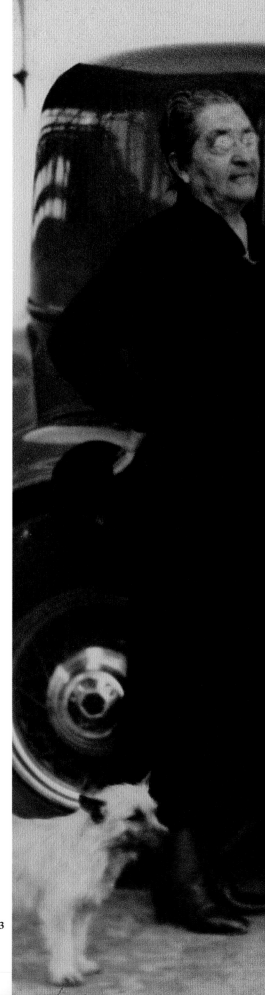

34

Miss Helen Mary Campbell

My mother was born Helen Mary Campbell on April 4, 1902, in Pittsburg, Kansas. She was five feet, seven inches tall and had beautiful brown eyes, auburn hair, and a fair complexion. She seldom wore powder or lipstick and never rouge.

She loved horses and started riding when she was very young. She began driving her parents' electric car when she was twelve and was a good mechanic. She enjoyed being outdoors, playing polo, riding for fun, and going fox hunting in Pennsylvania, Maryland, Delaware, and Virginia. Her equestrian skills earned her an excellent reputation among area military officers, whom she often represented in horse shows. An entry in her journal reported, "Colin came home last Friday and Margaret came the next day. I went to Ft. Myer to a drill in the afternoon and a tea dance afterwards." In addition to riding, my mother played tennis and golf, attended luncheons and dances, shopped, went on picnics, went to movies, and read many books.

MY MOTHER'S JOURNALS

Like her father, my mother began at an early age to keep detailed accounts of her thoughts and activities. She was a private person. When she was fifteen, she began documenting her life. As the years passed, these journals included our family activities, Daddy's work, and many of her personal feelings. Her entries, which she continued until early 1963, shortly before she died, have aided in the reconstruction of my parents' lives.

In early 1917, the United States was not yet at war with Germany. Talk of a great global conflict was at the center of conversation in Washington. My mother's older brother, Colin, was attending the Naval Academy when she wrote, on March 27: "As the war calls for more naval officers, the first class graduated in March, instead of June. Colin was one of the star men and very proud of himself for the fact. They got four days leave and Brady, Colin's roommate, came up and spent his leave here."

A few days later, the United States declared war on Germany and we were in World War I. On May 3, my mother wrote of a wonderful experience she had while visiting the U.S. House of Representatives: "I stayed home from school to go down to the House and see the French Commission. Papa only had two tickets for the gallery so he took me in on the floor. When Monsieur Viviani finished speaking the Congressmen went around to shake hands with the others. When it came my turn the Admiral of the Navy and Viviani kissed my hand, but Marshall Joffre kissed my forehead. That was a great day for me and you may be sure, I never will forget it as long as I live!"

Mother's spirit of adventure, as is clear from her journal, occasionally conflicted with her father's wishes. On June 26, 1917, she wrote: "Saturday night we came home to get dressed and go to the dance in Alexandria and Papa told us we were not going. Sunday morning we went to church in the electric car. In the afternoon we stayed home, because the boys went on a picnic. They came back here about 6:30, to go down to the Carter's, but Papa wouldn't let us go with them."

Mother's writings tell of her many and varied experiences, including what would develop into a life-long love of photography: "Tuesday, I took the car in to have the starter fixed in the morning and went around to see Mary a minute. I took a lot of pictures of her and every one of them turned out fine."

VILLA MARIA

In a February 1918 entry, she wrote of a likely change in her future while attending Western High School in Washington, D.C.:

Helen Campbell, circa 1926

I passed in everything at school, for which everybody was very thankful, including yours truly, and I am doing pretty well now, not famous though. I don't like geometry very much! I am doing pretty well in my drawing. I got 8 credits in English, 7 in French and 7 in Algebra, so if I keep up the present record of good marks, I will be up in all of my credits. It may not make much difference though, whether I am up or not, as ten chances to one, I will be going to the Convent next year. We will probably motor out home [Kansas] next spring and I will go to the convent from there.

My mother's parents thought she was majoring in boys and was pretty wild, so they did send her to Villa Maria, a French convent school in Montreal. Villa Maria presented her with a drastic cultural change. She told me that the French girls did not bathe because they thought water was bad for their skin. They would run water in the bathtub, move their hands around in it, dry them quickly, and put on cream. Aside from the culture shock, my mother's experience at the convent changed her life. She was in the chapel, kneeling in prayer when a bright ball of light flashed through the sanctuary, entering one window and streaking out another. As a result of this phenomenon, she became very religious.

ADVENTURE IN WASHINGTON

After about a year, my mother returned to Washington and entered the National Cathedral School, an Episcopalian school for girls. She graduated in 1922, following in the footsteps of her sister Elizabeth, who had graduated in 1918.

When my mother was thirteen, the family had moved to Windsor. They loved its serenity and the views of the U.S. Capitol building and the Potomac River. Windsor was the center of numerous social and political activities for my grandfather, and Granny enjoyed hosting family and friends. The library was full of excellent photographs of government leaders, which my grandfather collected and prized.

During these years, my mother met many interesting people, resulting in some wonderful opportunities. She was sixteen when such an occasion presented itself: "The Princess David came to dinner on Sunday, and asked me to go back to Honolulu with her this summer. Well, I have fought and pleaded and gone to one place and then another, trying to get there, but papa said as usual 'No'! I have never known that man to make an affirmative answer in his life! I realize that I have missed the opportunity of a lifetime and whether or not it will come again, I do not know, but I sincerely hope so." My mother explained her dedication to her journals in a 1924 entry: "I have always found a great deal of pleasure reading chronicles of past years and so, years from now, I shall be able to read these, with much pleasure. I have had a very interesting life and as near as possible, should like to have some record of it."

In the mid-1920s, my mother accompanied her parents and her uncle John Campbell to London. Grandfather and his brother were attending an International Bar Association Convention. One evening John left his hotel to take a walk. When he did not return, a search ended tragically. His body was found floating in the murky waters of the Thames River. Mystery has forever shrouded this event; it was never known if my mother's uncle, then age fifty-five, accidentally fell or was pushed to his death.

Even as a youngster, my mother possessed a powerful sense of independence. She was adventurous, intelligent, organized, and detail-oriented. She inherited these qualities from her parents. As a young lady, she was popular in diplomatic and governmental circles. She was as much at home in the outdoors as she was at a formal party or serving as president of the Junior League of America. Her experiences prepared her well for whatever life would bring.

(following pages)
36 Helen Campbell at Western High School, Washington, D.C., 1918

37 Helen Campbell, 1920s

38 Helen Campbell with Windsor, circa 1935

39 Helen C. Kleberg at Saratoga, New York, circa 1940

36

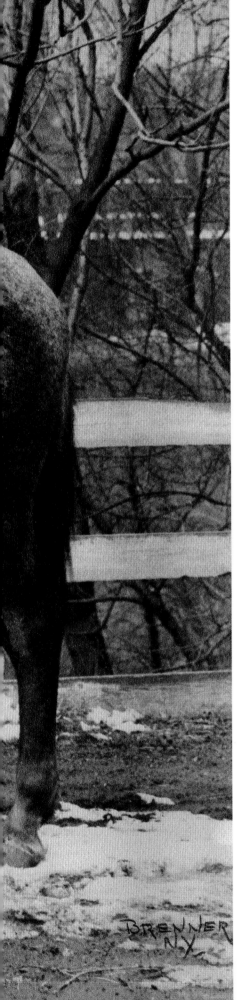

39

Bob Met Helen

True love and lifelong devotion

"The girl...you're going to marry."

Newlyweds Helen C. Kleberg and Bob Kleberg Jr. in Independence, Kansas, circa 1926

Drought and work had kept Bob Kleberg on the South Texas ranch for over two years. On February 2, 1926, after a long drive over unpaved roads, he arrived at the Saint Anthony Hotel in San Antonio. He telephoned his friend Mrs. Claude Hodges, whose husband Gen. John Hodges was stationed at Fort Sam Houston. Claude was an old ranch family friend of the Klebergs and always seemed to know where the action was.

"Hello, Bob," Mrs. Hodges said. "I've got the girl here that you're going to marry! Her name is Helen." She was referring to Helen Campbell, who had recently arrived in San Antonio to visit her sister Elizabeth and brother-in-law Burdette, and their two children. Burdette Shields Wright, an Army aviation officer stationed at Kelly Field, had distinguished himself in the skies over France during World War I, shooting down three enemy airplanes and becoming an Ace. The Wrights were already friends of my father. In fact, Mrs. Hodges had introduced my parents over the telephone earlier, but they had not met in person. My father loved my mother's voice.

My mother and Elizabeth had always been close. Their relationship became strained, however, as Elizabeth watched my mother seemingly "trifle with Bob's affections." Finally, out of frustration, she dragged my mother's travel trunk out to the sidewalk and exclaimed, "You must not lead my friend Bob Kleberg on like this! He does not understand this sort of thing. Stop it! Burdette and I have to go out tonight, and I want you to straighten this out by the time we get home. We will not put up with it."

Upon their return, they were greeted with big smiles from Helen and Bob. Helen told her older sister, "You have to call Father to tell him that Bob and I want to get married."

Astonished, Elizabeth said, "Why do I have to call? You're the ones wanting to get married."

"Well, you need to break the ice and let him know that nobody's dead and that nothing terrible has happened," my mother said. "Tell him Bob and I have some news. Then we'll talk to him."

Once her father was on the phone, Helen announced, "I want to marry Bob."

"Bob, who?" he said, after a pause.

My mother didn't even know how to spell Daddy's last name.

Grandfather Campbell asked him, "Bob, do you love Helen as much as I do?"

NO ACCIDENT

My mother's presence in San Antonio was not an accident. Earlier, a telegram from a gentleman had been delivered to her at Windsor. Her father was the first to read it: "Meet me under the clock at the Biltmore." I do not remember this fellow's name, but he continued, "Can't wait to see you. Love—."

Grandfather did not want his youngest daughter going to New York to meet this older man, who was in the diplomatic service. He knew she would insist on it, so he devised a plan. After Mother read the telegram, he said, "I know you'd like to go to New York, but I have an idea I believe you'll like even better. Here's a train ticket to San Antonio so you can visit your sister. Grandfather knew how close the two sisters were, so he knew a trip to Texas would be irresistible. It worked— my mother was as thrilled as if she had been given a ticket to Europe or the Orient.

Now, as Grandfather listened to the excitement in my mother's voice on the telephone, he realized that his plan had backfired. She had fallen in love and was asking his permission to marry a Texas rancher she had known only five days!

Many years later, when I was looking at old photographs with Granny Campbell, she recalled that from the time my mother was about twelve, she'd said she was going to marry someone who could give her horses. Then she added, "Your grandfather always worried about the wrong things."

HAPPY AS A FOOL

Quickly, Daddy, his friends, and his family went into action. First, Caesar Kleberg, my father's cousin who was in Washington on business, called on Grandfather Campbell. Daddy's best friend, Tom Armstrong, was the next to visit. Uncle Tom wore his "morning suit"—gray tails, striped pants, stock, and spats. He wanted to assure the former congressman that his future son-in-law's friends were not "country hicks." Afterward, Uncle Tom wrote Daddy, "Have called on Helen's father who introduced me to her mother and sister and have done my best to reassure them regarding you. Caesar and Roy trying to get a Resolution passed in Congress saying you are OK. Suggest you have Ma Ferguson call Texas legislature to take similar action. I await your further commands without prejudice."

My father's younger sister Sarah sent a telegram to Uncle Tom: "Bob is as happy as a fool. Looks like we will soon have another goat in the goat pen. I thoroughly approve and believe this is the best thing in the world for him. I know her slightly but like her because she speaks our language. Bob says she is one person he will never interrupt, so you know how sure he is. She got him and I'm glad of it!"

Within a few days, my mother received the following from Tom: "I have always considered [Bob] the champion and if you have him on his knees, the diamond belt is yours. Knowing Bob as I do, I extend my heartiest congratulations as well as my sincerest good wishes."

When my father returned to Santa Gertrudis to tell his parents the news, my mother wrote to him:

Please don't ever leave me any more. I have never spent such a long and miserable evening in my life. We have to carry on though, don't we? I'll try to manage some way but it won't be easy. You aren't in Kingsville yet but by the time this reaches you, the hardest part for you will be over.

My poor family to get such a shock in the middle of the night! I wrote to them trying to put their minds at ease, but unless they will take my word for it, they won't be greatly reassured. I could only tell them how wonderful you are, and how happy you have made me!

I've been told this was the only time my parents were apart during their short engagement.

The sun had long since set when my mother and her companions arrived at Santa Gertrudis. She wrote:

I shall never forget my first glimpse of the many bright stars overhead and the many lights rising out of the prairie. I braced myself to get out of the car into a new world, but no, that wasn't the house, it was the commissary. I had to brace myself again to do it all over again. This time we were at the door of a house built along the same lines as the commissary, square and two storied, with a tower but a much broader one. That was as much as I could make out in the dark. Then things started to happen. In spite of the lateness of the hour, people appeared from everywhere.

Shortly after this gathering, another reception was held at Santa Gertrudis for Congressman Campbell, who had come to meet my father. Upon Grandfather's arrival, Uncle Tom offered him a drink and he took it. I'm sure he needed it! And though they were of seemingly different cultures, they were laughing, joking, and drinking whiskey before the sun rose.

Normally, wedding ceremonies are held in or near the bride's home. Due to Grandfather Kleberg's poor health, however, and the fact that Mana would never leave his side, there was no way to have a wedding in Virginia. Daddy's best man, Tom Armstrong, was to leave soon for Argentina to assume his duties with Standard Oil. It was also time for Grandfather Campbell to return to Virginia, all of which added to the difficulty of scheduling the wedding day.

A SECRET PLAN

Unbeknownst to my parents and almost everyone else, Uncle Tom, Aunt Elizabeth, and Aunt Sarah had a plan. Tom and Elizabeth went to the Kleberg County courthouse in Kingsville to pick up the marriage license. Meanwhile, as Sarah drove down Leopard Street in Corpus Christi, she noticed a sign in a store window that read, "Gran Barata, wedding rings, half price." She bought a simple gold band. The Jones girls found a minister. Everyone but my Kleberg grandparents went to Corpus Christi for a final farewell to Congressman Campbell. It had been arranged that they would all meet in Uncle Dick's home, which Mrs. King had given him.

At last, when everything was in place, the group approached Grandfather for his permission to have the ceremony. After he agreed, they announced, "Phil Campbell will give his daughter away before leaving on the night train for Washington."

A small gathering, made up of close friends and family, assembled in Uncle Dick's Victorian house. My mother and Aunt Elizabeth were wearing riding breeches, boots, and twin green jackets. When my mother noticed that her sister's jacket was cleaner, she borrowed it. I don't know about something blue, but she did have something borrowed. My parents were married on March 2, 1926, by Pastor Jesus Cadena. Afterward, they attended a wedding breakfast and reception at the Nueces Hotel, hosted by the Jones family. Then the newlyweds departed with a picnic hamper filled with champagne, fruit, and other goods.

It truly was love at first sight. Leaving Corpus Christi, they motored to Armstrong Ranch. Aunt Lucy Armstrong remarked, "The bride and groom were not seen for three days, even though the plumbing in the cottage was not working."

PARALLEL LIVES

It may appear that my parents, who came from such different worlds and knew each other for only a short time before marrying, yet there were parallels.

The Klebergs, Kings, and Campbells, upon arriving in this country, spoke different languages and came from different cultures. All wanted to escape oppression and make their new alliance to a free country. All felt the lure of the West, with its opportunities to start new lives on open lands. A strong Protestant faith, self-confidence, family, and friends helped the families deal with privation, disease, shipwrecks, Indians, wars, and more.

Daniel Campbell and Richard King learned mathematics in "the school of hard knocks" and learned to read from the Bible. Robert Kleberg I had been a judge in Germany but did not hesitate to do manual labor. The wives of these men bore many children—somehow feeding them, looking after their health, spinning and weaving clothes for all, and educating them. Somehow, with next to nothing, they made homes and close-knit families.

They all learned English. The next generation worked and studied diligently. Philip Campbell and Robert Justus Kleberg II both became lawyers, as did several of their brothers. Philip met Rudolf Kleberg in Washington when both served in Congress. Rudolf's son, Caesar, and Philip enjoyed each other's company. In both families, love of the land, nature, and animals were ever present. All wished for a better life for their children and that, in turn, those children would be well-educated, good citizens serving family and country.

That legacy continued with my parents.

(preceding page)
40 Helen C. Kleberg and Bob Kleberg Jr., shortly after they were married

(facing page)
41 Honeymooners, Bob Kleberg Jr. and Helen C. Kleberg at La Bavia ranch, Coahuila, Mexico, circa 1926

(following pages)
42 Bob Kleberg Jr. and Helen C. Kleberg, circa 1926

43 Helen C. Kleberg and Bob Kleberg Jr. having fun, 1930s

44 Helen C. Kleberg and Bob Kleberg Jr. touring in Mexico on their honeymoon, late 1920s

HCK+RJK

43

Genetics

Developing the Santa Gertrudis, the Quarter Horse, and the best grazing grasses

King Ranch bred

From the beginning, King Ranch has explored, and often been at the forefront of, ways to increase cattle productivity. The effort toward improvement—with the overall goal of producing more digestible meat or protein from the available grass—began in 1878 with the introduction of the British breeds. In 1878, Captain King bought British-bred Hereford and Shorthorn bulls to upgrade his Longhorns for the changing times he foresaw. The adaptable, nearly indigenous Longhorns had served him well when their hides and tallow were all that could be sold. Later, their ability to walk to distant markets, fattening along the way, made them valuable.

After Captain King's death, Grandfather Kleberg brought in many prize bulls. By the time he was four years old, Daddy was seeing them arrive plump and shiny, but soon they were panting in the heat, feverish with ticks. They withered and died in spite of every care. The normally hot, dry weather conditions on the ranch, along with numerous insect pests, created an environment that was simply too harsh for the British breeds to prosper. The lack of predictable rainfall compounded the uncertainty: there might be water and no grass, or plenty of grass but no water for the livestock.

Daddy wrote that beef production on King Ranch "is a story of continuous effort and experimentation with different types and breeds. The purebreds multiplied until, by 1900, they stocked the entire ranch. Differences were noted between the Herefords and Shorthorns. The

Robert J. Kleberg Sr. (center) and Hereford bull, circa 1902

Herefords proved better rustlers and were more prolific on the stronger lands, while the Shorthorns weighed heavier and produced sturdier calves on the sandy soils. Prolonged drought, screwworms, ear ticks, and fever ticks took their toll on both breeds."[27]

ENVISIONING THE DREAM

During the time the ranch was seeing how different breeds did on the coastal plain, the ranch management was improving the pastures and watering places and gaining experience in handling livestock in South Texas. Both factors paved the way for the creation of the Santa Gertrudis breed.

Daddy said the ingredient that added adaptability to the breed was the introduction of Brahman blood into the herds. In 1910, Tom O'Connor gave the ranch a half-bred Shorthorn Brahman bull, which was turned into pasture with Shorthorn cows. "The crossbred cows from this and similar matings demonstrated their superiority immediately. . . . It was evident that these were the best range cattle seen on the property up to this time," Daddy wrote.[28]

Despite the fact that the crossbred cows' superiority was clear, their introduction was not without some discussion within the family. Daddy explains: "My mother especially admired the uniform red color in the Shorthorn herds, and upon seeing the brindle and black cows and calves, told me, 'I hate to see the red cattle go.' She lived to see the Santa Gertrudis in pasture all around her home and I would tell her, 'Well, Mother, you got your red cattle back.' "[29]

For the most part, the family, especially Daddy's generation, supported the cross-breeding effort. As his brother-in-law, Tom East, replied to a visitor's inquiry about the wildness of the Brahman at that time, "I'd a lot rather say yonder they go than there they lay."[30]

Daddy, who had grown up on the ranch working with the various cattle, came home from the University of Wisconsin with Alvin Sanders' book, *History of the Shorthorn Breed*. He had studied the methods Sanders discussed for development of the Shorthorn, as well as the latest scientific developments in genetics. (He would miss discussing this topic with his longtime friends, Howard Rouse of Midway, Kentucky, and Herbert Shipman of Hilo, Hawaii.)

Daddy used to say to me, "You must have a dream first. Then work like hell to make it come true." In his mind, he had set the criteria for the new breed he envisioned. It must be suited to the environment, must make good rustlers and mothers, must be cherry-red in color, and must be of good temperament, beefy, and early maturing.

With Uncle Dick's encouragement and his father's consent, Daddy acquired fifty-two Brahman bulls from A. P. Borden's herd. They were bred to 2,500 cows divided into eight herds. Two Brahman bulls, Chiltipin and Vinotero, were specifically selected and pasture mated to fifty cows each.

MONKEY

The next year, Uncle Dick, who was managing the Laureles division, called Daddy to come see a special calf, Monkey. His mother, a red "milk cow" that was one-sixteenth Brahman from the O'Connor bull and the rest Shorthorn, had produced a beautiful bull calf from her mating with Vinotero. Daddy agreed with his brother that this was the bull they were looking for.

Monkey's mother was a family milk cow at Laureles headquarters while she raised her cherry-red son. He was gentle, learning to lead readily. He and several other bull calves were sent to the Fort Worth stock show to be exhibited and sold. When Daddy found out, he convinced his father not to sell Monkey.

Monkey was the "prepotent sire" my father was hoping to find. He wrote, "For many years, only Monkey, his sons, grandsons, great-grandsons, daughters, granddaughters, and great-granddaughters have been used. In the original work, Monkey was mated to both first-cross and double-cross heifers. In all cases, they were carefully selected. They were the best individuals available, all red in color. Staying within one family wrought a steady improvement in the breed."[31]

COMBINATION BREEDING PLANS

Breeding selected sons of Monkey in single sire herds, Daddy soon identified the best breeder that in turn was used in a single sire herd. Santa Gertrudis was the best son of Monkey. Soon there were enough sons of one of the good bulls to be able to use their half-brothers in multiple sire herds, thus rapidly increasing numbers.

Careful records were kept on 300 cows divided into nine or ten single sire herds. I remember Daddy explaining good and bad points of calves and their mothers, including similarities between them. As we got a cow with her calf in the *calera* round pen and drove the pair into the chute, Daddy would call out a grade ranging from A to D. Each cow and calf was weighed. The calves were branded to denote parentage, and then they were vaccinated and the bulls of poor conformation or color were castrated. Weight, age, color, and grade were recorded for each cow. With these meticulous records, it was possible to tell in a few years not only how a cow was producing, but also how many calves were good enough for bulls and how many daughters each bull had.

Monkey, circa 1928

Bob Kleberg Jr. receiving honorary Ph.D. from Texas A&M University in recognition of his life's work in cattle breeding, 1940

Dr. J. K. Northway, King Ranch chief veterinarian who worked closely with Bob Kleberg in the development of Santa Gertrudis, circa 1950

Several sons of each bull that was considered extra good could be tested in these single sire herds. Monkey's best sons were Santa Gertrudis I, II, and III; Santa Gertrudis's best were Tipo, Coton, and Rapido. Several sons from one family would be bred to daughters of another bull, always tracing back to Monkey.

Soon Daddy designed single-sire, multiple-sire herd combination breeding plans, which at that time were unique in large-scale breeding. He wrote, "Most of these bulls in turn, the produce of the small multiple sire herds, were sent to the commercial herds. This system allowed the King Ranch to quickly take advantage of superior beef production of the Santa Gertrudis breed."[32]

If any female from the 300-cow registry did not seem up to standard as a cow or calf, she went to market, not into a lesser commercial herd. Daddy found that breeding cross-breds to cross-breds led to more diversity and less uniformity. It was intense selection, using inbreeding and line-breeding, that could result in uniformity. The "bad individuals" from inbreeding were culled as calves. Daddy culled "poor doers" on the range in time of drought. He never "creep fed" calves. If the herd needed feed, they all got equal opportunity, although sometimes for years it was cactus seared by a pear burner and two pounds of cottonseed cake. The "good doers" would multiply in good years.

The road to the Santa Gertrudis breed was rough in spots. Brucellosis got into several herds, causing "contagious abortion." Once a cow had aborted, she would breed and not abort, in a kind of self-vaccina-

Bob Kleberg Jr. inspecting grass in Australia, 1956

tion. A plan of weaning calves early, before puberty, was implemented. Those calves went to "clean ground" and were mated only to their age peers after all had been tested. Soon there was a brucellosis vaccine for females. The disease has been almost completely eradicated in the United States.

Unfortunately, the carefully kept records on the Santa Gertrudis breed, the ranch horses, and the Jersey herd went up in flames when the office of the King Ranch veterinarian, Dr. J. K. Northway, burned to the ground in the mid-1930s. B. K. Johnson and I rode up to see what we could find—maybe a spatula or a nail—but only ashes remained. Luckily, between the memories of the Kineños, Dr. Northway, and my mother and father, much was reconstructed.

FIRST TRULY AMERICAN BREED

In 1940, Daddy's brother, Congressman Richard Kleberg, with the help of Dr. W. H. Black of the USDA Beef Cattle Division of the U.S. Department of Agriculture, took the unprecedented step of recognizing King Ranch–bred genetics. The Santa Gertrudis is a pure breed, the first so designated in the Western hemisphere.

Daddy said, "While the art of breeding requires intense application to detail, endless study, observation, and application of a keen artistic sense, the rewards are great and I know of no task of such consuming and lasting interest."[33]

My daughter Emory recalls, "Grandfather recognized the need for a source of protein to feed the people of many undeveloped countries. Thus, his life's work had one common element—the plan to use marginal areas, not fertile lands, to create protein."

GRASS TO PROTEIN

Grass is the basic food for cattle and horses, whether in its green stage or dry as hay. Good grass depends on good soil, and some of it on high moisture.

As a boy, Daddy saw the effects of drought, insects, and overgrazing. He used the wonderful monoculture Rhodes grass pastures in later years for the single-sire Santa Gertrudis herds in the 1930s and for fattening thousands of steers on the new plantations at Laureles during World War II. Suddenly, that wonderful grass was gone, leaving bare ground with a few grass termite structures around dead stems. A "bug" that made the grass joints bleed destroyed every plant.

With the aid of agronomist Nicholas Diaz, the search for palatable native grasses began. Seed was gathered from the better plants, and a grass breeding and selection program was implemented. Grasses from other states and countries were also introduced. These grasses had to be nutritious, palatable, and drought and disease resistant. Frances Fugate documented some of this work in his book *The Grass Program*, with input from Daddy and Nicholas Diaz.

In the smaller pastures around the Santa Gertrudis headquarters, Daddy insisted on pasture rotation. In the larger, sandy pastures and the coastal plain, he did not allow overstocking. He did not believe in burning on the sandy soils; a mulch or standing vegetation protected sprouting seeds from the extremes of heat and cold of the fine white sand. He lived by the old ranch credo, "Take care of your country, and it will take care of you."

John Cypher, who often traveled with or for my father after my mother died, recalled how Daddy ordered him to arrange for shipment of seed for newly cleared land at Monstrenco, one of our ranches in Venezuela: "It was an example of taking advantage of our experience in one country to solve a problem in another."[34]

In 1973, the year before Daddy's last safari, the African Safari Club of Washington, D.C., honored him with their seventh annual National Conservation Award. A portion of the award stated:

> Robert J. Kleberg Jr. developed detailed programs for game management and conservation practices over many years of trial and error on the King Ranch and on other large holdings in Australia and South America. He developed the Santa Gertrudis cattle, a breed which can be successfully raised in subtropical climates. In 1967, he established a research center at Texas A&M University and put the resources of the Caesar Kleberg Research Program in Wildlife Ecology, of which he is President, into the project. He traveled extensively in East Africa and obtained first-hand information about the conflicting as well as the complementary needs of people and wildlife. . . . It is doubtful, however, if any one man, any time, anywhere, has ever made a greater personal contribution to the acquisition of knowledge and proper development of the animal and plant resources of this one world.

Daddy knew that you must build on your experiences and knowledge to be successful. In the case of grasses, he made sure the results of constant research were utilized to improve the nutritional output of the grasses being grazed by King Ranch cattle and horses. He led the way in this stewardship effort.

(preceding pages)
45 Hereford cow and Africander bull at King Ranch, 1933

(following pages)
46 Brahman cows with Charolais calves, 1941

47 Crystal herd at King Ranch, 1944

48 Santa Gertrudis herd

49 Bob Kleberg Jr. and Peter Baillieu standing in field of Lucerne (alfalfa), 1956

50 Bob Kleberg Jr. looking at Guinea grass, Australia, 1953

51 Moving a great herd of horses on King Ranch, circa 1940

50

51

King Ranch horses

Since the days of Captain King, good horses have been a major part of King Ranch's production. Those not needed on the ranch were easily sold. Although Grandfather Kleberg was not particularly noted for his equestrian skills, he had an appreciation of good horses. His and Alice's children rode from infancy, becoming accomplished riders. Grandfather Kleberg introduced considerable Thoroughbred blood, though not always producing the desired results.

OLD SORREL

In 1916, when Daddy returned from the University of Wisconsin, he wanted to apply the scientific methods he had learned to improve the ranch's horses. The criteria to be met included soundness, smoothness, cow sense, gentleness, tractability, strength, stamina, and the ability to maintain condition as well as peers under the same circumstances. It's important to remember that ranch horses had to live in the country with seldom a whiff of oats or hay. All of these traits had to be tested.

Caesar Kleberg, Daddy's cousin, friend, and confidant who had come to work for the ranch after his father's term in Congress ended, took young Bob to meet George Clegg, a "horse friend." Daddy was enchanted with a small band of beautiful uniform chestnut mares, which Clegg referred to as his "wax dolls." One colt particularly drew his and Caesar's attention. They came home with Old Sorrel, which would become the patriarch of King Ranch horses and the American Quarter Horse breed.

My father remembered Old Sorrel as the best cow horse he ever rode on the ranch. He said, "He was exceptional as to beauty, disposition, conformation, smoothness of action and fine handling qualities."[35] To settle an argument between my parents, my cousin, Dick Kleberg Jr., home on vacation from Virginia Military Institute, jumped Old Sorrel bareback with only a halter to guide

him over rails set at four feet in the Hitchcock corral. Daddy took Old Sorrel up and down the stairs in the twenty-one-foot-ceiling commissary with ease, raced him, cut on him, and roped off him, and I rode him "loose" when I was four.

Old Sorrel was bred to the best fifty mares on the ranch. Daddy said they were mostly purebred Thoroughbreds or part Thoroughbreds. Solis and Tino were both from Ed Lazarus' St. Simon line Thoroughbreds. (Daddy was crazy about Martin's Best, a stallion from the same line, which he rode as a young man. He liked Martin's Best's breeding, so he bought every mare Mr. Lazarus offered to the ranch.)

Daddy also said the first effort at concentrating and preserving the blood was made when Solis was mated to his own daughters from the same band of mares. He was then mated to forty of his half-sisters, mostly from Thoroughbred mares. Old Sorrel became the "Monkey" and Solis became the "Santa Gertrudis" of horses—an excellent horse for ranch work, polo, fox hunting, military use, or pleasure riding.

AMERICAN QUARTER HORSE

After conversations with Wayne Densmore of the Horse and Mule Association and a meeting with several prominent rancher horsemen, it was decided, at my parents' dinner table, that these good horses needed a registry similar to the one for Thoroughbreds.

To pick the number one horse for the new American Quarter Horse Association registry, the ranchers were invited to bring their best stallions for a class to be judged by several top horsemen. Wimpy, son of Solis, became Wimpy P-1 and was judged the ideal horse for the association, becoming the association's first regis-

Bob Kleberg Jr. working with a foal to improve his stance, 1943

Wimpy P-1, in foreground, the ideal of the American Quarter Horse breed, and his *manada*, at Santa Gertrudis, circa 1940

tered horse. Peppy won the 1941 Grand Champion Stallion in Tucson, Arizona, and from him are descended Mr. San Peppy and Peppy San Badger, which are so influential today in the American Quarter Horse breeding lineage.

As for Tino, Daddy used to cut on his full brother with no bridle in big herds on the open range to show off to guests. I was asked to show some beautiful mares that were smooth, quick, and "cowy," and that could jump backward.

All of Old Sorrel's stallion descendants that were used for breeding on the ranch were tested for roping and cutting, as were the mares. This was not the case on most ranches. Daddy insisted that before King Ranch mares were bred, they had to perform. This was to eliminate bad tempers, bad feet, poor bone, and any other negative trait that could be genetically passed on. He also checked to see if each mare was a poor mover, if she was rough, and if she could keep up with the others being raised on the same country, without requiring extra feed.

In addition, because horses raised on King Ranch would be subject to sand burn, the white was bred out of them. We later brought the white back with Little Peppy. There were other exceptions; we had some palominos and some grays. But Daddy's favorite color was chestnut, with bay being second. He liked these colors because they always looked good, even when the horses were turned out all the time.

I had a daughter of Old Sorrel to use when I went fox hunting at Foxcroft. My children hunted on Australian Welsh ponies and then King Ranch Quarter Horses. They won prizes in hunter classes as well.

Starting in the early 1950s, King Ranch held sales of Quarter Horse yearlings and Santa Gertrudis bulls. Thus the breeds' genetics were spread all over the country and to many other lands.

ROVALO

Daddy gave my mother Rovalo, a big horse that she loved in spite of his quirks. Among them was the fact that he could not be bridled until he had been saddled. Rovalo could be out in the pasture, sound asleep under a tree, but the minute he was saddled he started stomping his feet and was ready to go. During a field trial in the Laguna Larga Pasture at Santa Gertrudis, something spooked Rovalo, causing him to run off with my mother. A retired Texas Ranger noticed and jumped into his car. He raced across the pasture in pursuit. This petrified my mother, who was fearful he would turn in front of them and cause a terrible accident. She never rode Rovalo again. My cousin Dick Kleberg Jr. got along fine with Rovalo and cut many cattle on him.

SPIRIT OF AMERICA

Daddy's appreciation of horses prompted him to write an article in 1941 for *The Cattleman*, titled "The Horse and His Place in Present Day Life." He felt that horses were central to American ideals and culture.

The horse is not in competition with the automobile, the streamliner and the airplane. His day is done in the scheme of popular transportation, and far be it from me to recommend a groping return to the much maligned horse and buggy days. I don't mean that at all. . . . Such great natural appeal has the horse that people, regardless of class, creed, occupation or social position, are instantly taken from the grooves of their work-a-day existence and given a common ground for recreation and discussion when he appears on the scene.[36]

Daddy also discussed the importance of the organizations like the American Quarter Horse Association, saying:

"They are destined not only to stimulate the public's interest in horses, but to improve the horses themselves, in breeding, handling, training and supply. . . . The public is entitled to expect and to be provided with a high-class product, and that product should be so bred, developed and schooled that the public will not be disappointed. . . . Give America her boots and her saddles; and her soul will go marching on."[37]

(following pages)

52 Wimpy, in foreground, with his *manada* (mare band)

53 Pepino with remuda at Santa Gertrudis, 1943

54 Quarter Horse culling at Telephone Pens, Laureles division, King Ranch, 1944

55 Richard (Dick) Kleberg Jr. and Agostín Quintanilla shaping remuda, 1944

56 Bob Kleberg Jr. with mares, circa 1941

57 Richard (Dick) Kleberg Jr. inspecting remuda at Santa Gertrudis, 1944

54

57

My Mother's Muse

Capturing and recording the unique action
and beauty of King Ranch

A love of the arts

Throughout her life, my mother enjoyed sketching and painting, as her journal shows: "Spent the day in the car doing watercolors of roundup—principally a man wearing a yellow slicker against the pretty sky and brown grass." She occasionally sketched portraits and scenes she remembered from her travels in Mexico. She also painted in oils, inspired by her artist friend from San Antonio, Mary Aubrey Keating, who worked primarily in watercolors.

My mother was fond of the work of a Mexican folk artist known as Corona. She bought several tiny wooden chests and a tray on which he had painted deer, colonial-era human figures, trees, and birds. Inspired by these objects, she painted similar designs on the sliding doors in her and my father's bathroom. She also painted a Mexican folk mural in the camp house at the Martillo as well as furniture.

My mother had a great design sense and enjoyed the artistic process. She made detailed plans for Norias with Daddy's input, and she taught me the basics of proportion and what was essential to a house or garden plan. She said you shouldn't ask anyone to do what you don't know how to do yourself, and she enjoyed figuring out how to do the art projects she was interested in. Another thing she often said was, "Make where you live home." She sewed gauze curtains for our living room and skirts of plain muslin for her simple dressing table. She decorated them with drawings of birds that she made with crayons, ironing the designs to fix the color in the fabric. She also made a canopy of peau de soie, complete with a rosette in the center, for the four-poster bed she had found in Matamoros, Mexico. This was a difficult job, as she had to work from a pattern book on the cramped floor of an unair-conditioned room. This project was more difficult than the sofa and chair covers she made for our living room.

My mother loved art. She had studied modern art in the early 1940s with help from a friend, Nelson Rockefeller. One of her favorite artists was the Australian painter William Dobell, regarded by many as Australia's greatest portraitist. Dobell's paintings received three Archibald Prizes and the Wynne Prize, and he was greatly appreciated by Prince Philip, who commissioned him to paint *Country Race Meeting* and *Beach Carnival* and placed the works in the private rooms of Windsor Castle. Dobell was knighted in 1966. The August 4, 1962, *Australian Daily Telegraph* reported:

> An American cattle rancher's wife yesterday bought a small William Dobell oil painting for 1350 guineas at a Sydney auction. She is Mrs. Robert J. Kleberg, wife of the president of the King Ranch in Texas. Mrs. Kleberg bought the painting on her first bid. The 7-inch by 11-inch painting, *Boy Sunbathing*, was one of 13 paintings by Australian artists auctioned by Geoff K. Gray Pty, Ltd.[38]

The painting was the sixth she owned by this artist; she'd bought the others on a visit to Australia a decade earlier.

Bob Kleberg Jr. and Helen C. Kleberg as always with her camera, 1950s

Music of all kinds, opera, ballet, and theater were a joy to my mother. Daddy loved Caruso and Mexican music along with musicals and theater.

PHOTOGRAPHY

Through her photography, my mother told the story of her life with my father. Although she had started taking pictures in her early teens and continued to use a Brownie camera for years afterward, her true photographic interest matured when she got a Leica in the 1930s. She was enthralled with the self-expression photography permitted and had a good eye for composition. Because of her devotion to my father and her admiration for his life's work, she took thousands of color slides and black-and-white images of him and life on the ranch over the years. Using natural light and positioning, she captured beautiful outdoor scenes of ranch activities that included Daddy cutting, roping, and working with the vaqueros as they rounded up great herds of cattle and horses. She also composed many close-ups of individual animals, family members, friends, and visitors.

Detail-oriented and organized, my mother tirelessly labeled and categorized her slides. She wasn't just taking pictures; she was creating a historical record, which she assembled in three-ring binders that combined photographs with letters of recommendation regarding King Ranch cattle and horses. She also captured thousands of images of ranch and Thoroughbred horses, facilities, hunting scenes, and family gatherings around the world. Many of her slides were used in early King Ranch sales catalogs. She developed many of these pictures in my bathtub at Santa

Gertrudis. Often I couldn't go into my bedroom, let alone the bathroom, until I had her permission. Later she got her own darkroom.

Photography for my mother was a labor of love that spanned the early 1930s through the early 1960s. Her work reached a critical turning point in 1939. Late that year, I went with my parents to Corpus Christi to see *Gone With the Wind*. This epic motion picture of the South during the Civil War, which was shot in Technicolor, had a profound effect on my mother's work. After she saw it, she began using color slide film. In the summer of that year, my parents met the well-known fashion photographer Toni Frissell while they were at the track at Saratoga, New York. Their friendship would provide my mother, who was basically self-taught, with a great opportunity to learn photography from one of America's best-known photographers.

TONI FRISSELL

Toni Frissell was very artistic and loved the outdoors. I do not know who introduced her to my parents, but it's plain that they hit it off right away. I believe Toni recognized a great opportunity to expand her outdoor portfolio by capturing images of King Ranch and its people. I'm sure she realized that my parents represented the greatest livestock entity in America. And, like Toni, my mother loved art and the outdoors and had a keen photographic eye. There must have been a natural bond between the two from the start.

My parents invited Toni to the ranch, and over the next five years she visited many times, capturing the King Ranch culture on film. Before that, she had been the first to use the outdoors as a backdrop for photographing fashion models. Her photographs first appeared in *Vogue* and *Harper's Bazaar* during the 1930s. Though she is perhaps best known for her pioneering fashion photography, in later years she also photographed subjects as diverse as the Berlin Wall and the 1968 Republican National Convention.

Toni Frissell photographed the King Ranch from many vantage points, circa 1939

By the time Toni finished her work at the ranch in 1944, she had created 40,000 color transparencies and 270,000 black-and-white negatives that were eventually presented to the Library of Congress. Reflecting on her trips to Texas, she said, "As I drove toward the ranch, my heart beat a little faster in anticipation of the various experiences I was to encounter and record. There was never a greater studio that a photographer had the privilege in which to work."[39] Of her photography of ranch life, she said:

> On the days of round ups we'd get up early, very early—three or four o'clock in the morning. In summer the sun in Texas comes up very early (and hot) . . . we were waked by a cup of coffee served at bedside at the Santa Gertrudis Division headquarters . . . then we got in a car. At that time there were not many roads and we would drive forty, fifty, sixty miles to the round up . . . As the round up work got underway, Bob and one or two of the most experienced vaqueros would ride into the herd, very quietly.[40]

After her work at King Ranch, Toni traveled the world, photographing Sir Winston Churchill and Lady Churchill, the Duke and Duchess of Marlborough, and other well-known figures. Her informal portraits of the famous and powerful in the United States and Europe would become another of her landmark contributions to photography. During World War II she documented Red Cross workers, airmen, orphaned children, soldiers, and numerous other protagonists in this conflict. She photographed personalities such as Elizabeth Taylor; Mary Martin; Lilli Palmer and Rex Harrison; Baron Guy de Rothschild and his wife, Gloria Vanderbilt; the John Jacob Astor children; President Franklin D. Roosevelt; and President and Mrs. John F. Kennedy. In addition, she recorded many wonderful outdoor scenes, including fox hunts, mountain climbers, and snow skiers. She photographed my wedding in 1949. A finer present no one could have!

My mother "captured" Toni Frissell, as well, both on horseback and perched high on the windmill towers she frequently climbed to obtain grand vistas of cattle and horses on the vast landscape. Toni, known as Mrs. Francis Bacon in private life, shared many of her techniques with my mother:

1. Catch the subject at an instant of pleasure or emotion.
2. Know your subject's interests beforehand.
3. Click your camera at typewriter speed. Film is a cheap commodity.
4. Luck—the commodity that puts one at a crucial event and the chance is given of recording a vital instant.[41]

She also taught my mother the importance of proper lens and light. In addition to Toni, my mother enjoyed visiting and corresponding with several other well-known female photographers, including Gee Whitney, who later married Josiah Marvel Jr., ambassador to Denmark, and Grace Eustace. Closer to home, Dick Kleberg Jr., Leroy Denman, and John Cypher shared their interest.

62

Always Welcoming

Friends, family, researchers, artists, scholars,
and international visitors

"In wine there is friendship"

As I have said before, my parents grew up in families where hospitality was a grand tradition. The Kleberg motto was "In wine there is friendship," and to Daddy, friendship was almost a religion. My parents loved people and enjoyed extending their friendships around the world. Whether their visitors or guests were cattle buyers, royalty, top military officials, neighbors, friends, artists, or writers, they all sat at the table in our home or at camp. Some have said that my parents went out of their way to invite royal visitors to the ranch. But most of those guests came because of requests originating from leaders of government, military, business, family, or friends and then became friends.

Daddy was keenly aware of the importance of good public relations with people from around the world. Gustavo de los Reyes, who managed the King Ranch properties in Venezuela, observed: "Bob Kleberg invited Maria Gabriella, the princess of Savoy, to visit Venezuela. When she and her entourage arrived, they began spending lots of money and I noticed that they were putting it on Bob's account. I went to him and complained. His response to me was very clear: 'We are in the cattle business, Gustavo. These people are in the royal business. That's the way it is!' I had never heard anyone state it so exactly."

WILL ROGERS
On November 6, 1931, the *New York Times* quoted Will Rogers, the cowboy humorist, entertainer, and actor, as saying, "I did my best acting today—trying to look and act like a cowboy on Bob Kleberg's best cutting horse and hanging on by my teeth. Both Kleberg girls dragged calves up to the branding fire faster than I ever could. This is a real outfit. If you think there ain't any more real cowboys in this country, you're crazy."[42]

Rogers was a family friend. He visited often during roundups, as he loved to rope. I was four years old one time that he came, and I barely remember him, but I do recall his biplane landing in the horse pasture. I remember seeing men set up a roll of fence wire around the plane to keep the horses from eating the canvas wings. Apparently they liked the glue. Rogers was killed flying with Wiley Post in Alaska. His wife joined my parents during hunting season later.

LORD AND LADY HALIFAX
In early 1942, the admiral of the Corpus Christi Naval Base asked Daddy whether he would host Lord Halifax, the British ambassador to the United States, and Lady Halifax, on a tour of King Ranch. Daddy agreed, of course. When he told my mother, she had a slight panic, realizing there was no tea service in our house. She called Olga Weiss in Houston, a close friend whose husband, Harry, was president of Humble Oil and Refining Company.

"Do you think you could find me a tea service?" she asked. "There's no such thing in Kingsville." Olga telephoned my mother and said that, although no china was being imported, she had found a beautiful antique English tea service. "How perfect!" my mother said with relief. "Please have it packed and sent to Kingsville. I'll meet the bus. Send me the bill. Thank you ever so much."

Determined that everything would be done properly, she invited several friends, including Mrs. Lee Gillette, Daddy's secretary; Etta Larkin, a niece; and Mary Lewis Kleberg, Dick Kleberg Jr.'s wife, to our home to rehearse. Mary Lewis recalled:

Helen demanded perfection and would not settle for less. She said, "I don't know if anyone here knows about an English tea in the afternoon, so we are going to practice." She had us

From left: Lord Halifax, Henrietta Larkin, Lady Halifax, Tom Armstrong, unknown, and Bob Kleberg Jr. on new Norias porch, April 1947

practice in her dining room. We were shown how to pass everything including little sandwiches, cookies, and tea from a little teapot.

She wanted us to be able to take over in case the help slipped up. We got through the practice with everyone having fun.

The Halifaxes arrived at Santa Gertrudis in the afternoon on April 27. After the formal introductions, my mother said, "Lady Halifax, would you care for a cup of tea?"

"No, thank you, I never take tea," she said. "I would take a cup of coffee, if it isn't too much trouble."

My mother then asked, "Lord Halifax, would you care for tea?"

"No, thank you, but I would love a glass of cold water if you have it."

Needless to say, the sandwiches became appetizers and the tea was iced for the next day. The tea service sent by Olga Weiss remains in the corner cupboard, having been used only once, for the practice.

Shortly after the royal couple departed, Daddy received the following from Lord Halifax: "I can't tell you how grateful we were for your allowing us to be your guests on the Ranch. It was a great experience for us, and you and Mrs. Kleberg are the most perfect hosts . . . I was immensely impressed with everything that you showed us, both in the way of all your breeding operations and also in the management and handling of your immense herds." Lady Halifax wrote to my mother: "It was a perfectly delightful visit full of interest and pleasure from beginning to end—it only had one drawback to our minds and that was that it did not last longer!"

My parents and the Halifaxes became close friends, visiting for roundups and hunting. In a few years, my mother and father would visit them in England for racing at Newmarket and other occasions.

KING MICHAEL

On April 1, 1948, King Michael, formerly of Romania, arrived at the ranch. During World War II, he was influential in the overthrow of Romanian Gen. Ion Antonescu, who supported Hitler against the Russians. But when the war was over, the Russians entered Romania and King Michael was forced to abdicate his throne. He left the country in the late 1940s. Since that time, he has been referred to as the "King without a Country."

At the airport to greet the twenty-one-year-old king and his large entourage were Bobby Shelton, Aunt Henrietta Larkin, my mother, my father, Ila and Jim Clements, Dick and Mary Lewis Kleberg, a few others, and myself. My mother was ill in bed during most of King Michael's visit, but she had already determined the menus and arranged the seating. A certain amount of protocol and formality were required when greeting a royal guest. When she was instructing Mary Lewis on how to address the king and how to curtsy, Mary Lewis said, "I'm not going to bow to any king without a country!" She did, though.

King Michael was a charming young man who was interested in cars and airplanes. Daddy and I rode with him from Santa Gertrudis to Norias in a Lincoln Mark III. The handsome king drove at more than 100 mph over the unfinished highway. It was a miracle we didn't have a blowout. Daddy had bought two of these cars at the beginning of the war, as he knew he would need good transport, and cars for civilians were not being built. But that car was never the same after King Michael drove it!

For several days, my father escorted the king around the ranch, showing him some of our finest cattle and horses and treating his entourage to lavish meals at almost every stop. On the last day we went to Norias for a roundup. Willie Flores, who had been Caesar Kleberg's cook for many years, was the chief camp cook. His menu included everything that was part of a six-month-old heifer except for the hide and hooves. In addition, we dined on pinto beans, cabbage, sweet potatoes with oranges, and camp bread. A few hours later, we stopped at the new ranch house at Norias, which had been mostly designed by my parents

King Michael of Romania, circa 1948

Ambassador to the United Kingdom Louis Douglas, Bob Kleberg Jr., Princess Maria Gabriella of Savoy, 1950s

Bob Kleberg Jr. and Dean Rusk at American Assembly at Colombia University

Author and artist Tom Lea and Bob Kleberg Jr.

Mary and Nelson Rockefeller, 1940

a few years earlier. Waiting for us were irresistible appetizers of guacamole and chips, tiny Guatemalan enchiladas, quail salad tapas, and a variety of drinks.

It was getting late when we returned to Santa Gertrudis for a formal dinner. Joining the royal entourage in the big house were my mother and father, local ranchers, navy brass, family, and friends. The cooks were Texan, Mexican, Guatemalan, and German. They had prepared a sumptuous menu, including oysters in a creamy cheese sauce, Guatemalan enchiladas, Mexican enchiladas and tamales, roast beef with Yorkshire pudding, and crème bruleé. This was not what my mother had planned, but I believe the cooks thought this was their chance to show what they could do. During the meal, King Michael's aide stood and asked if he could be excused. He fainted dead away. The rich food, heat, and tight schedule had been too much.

KING OF MOROCCO

King Mohammed V of Morocco visited in 1957. John Cypher, longtime assistant to my father, recalled, "Over the years, King Ranch attracted a number of reigning and unemployed monarchs; Mohammed was the most regal, and possibly the most intelligent of them all." The *Cattleman* reported, "The monarch rode a Quarter Horse, inspected part of the ranch's Thoroughbred racing string, looked over top specimens of the Santa Gertrudis cattle and climbed into the cab of a big brush-clearing machine for a demonstration."[43]

QUEEN ELIZABETH

In the fall of 1957, my parents flew to Washington, D.C., to attend a reception honoring Queen Elizabeth II and Prince Philip at the British Embassy. Afterward, they motored with the royal party to an event hosted by Mr. and Mrs. Paul Mellon at the Middleburg Training Track in Virginia, where yearlings were presented for inspection. Our dear friend Anne Armstrong recalls, "The Queen Mother was just crazy about Bob Kleberg, and whenever Tobin and I would go to England, she always asked about him."

VISCOUNT AND VISCOUNTESS HARCOURT

In 1959, guests at the ranch included Mrs. Nelson Rockefeller, Viscount and Viscountess Harcourt (Bill and Betty) of Great Britain, Mr. and Mrs. Sam Hordern of Australia, and ex-president Gen. Pedro Aramburu of Argentina and his wife, as well as my mother's sister, Elizabeth.

The group spent the first few days at Norias and then returned to Santa Gertrudis to look at the cattle and horses, eat lunch around the pool, and go into Kingsville to shop in the King Ranch Store. Shortly after everyone left, my parents received news that Viscountess Harcourt had been hospitalized in New York City with a cerebral hemorrhage. My mother flew up to be with her, but her dear friend never recovered, dying on October 30.

My mother told Bill Harcourt that she was "grateful to God for having let her cross our paths for so short a time. We are all better, because Betty lived." After the funeral, my mother wrote in her journal, "Returned to Norias, tired, sad and wanting a cup of tea."

ELIZABETH ARDEN

My parents got to know Elizabeth Arden at the races. She stabled her racehorses next to King Ranch trainer Max Hirsch's barns at Belmont. She loved horses and had a beautiful horse farm in Kentucky. Her trainer in England, Capt. Boyd Rotchford, also trained the Queen of England's horses. Her Thoroughbred, Jet Pilot, won the 1947 Kentucky Derby. My mother enjoyed visiting with Ms. Arden at the races and had a lot of respect for her business acumen and for the wonderful cosmetics, perfumes, and shops she had put together worldwide.

Eight-Hour Cream was used for abrasions, and Arden Skin Lotion replaced horse liniment in Ms. Arden's racing stable. She gave Daddy some cream, and he used it on his hands when they got dry and chapped and on minor abrasions. He believed in it about as much as she did. Daddy was also fond of iodine for cuts or bruises. He said that if you had a bad bruise, painting the area with iodine would take out all the soreness.

BING CROSBY

Fellow rancher and close family friend Tobin Armstrong recalls that Bing Crosby and his wife would occasionally visit the ranch. "On one occasion, we met for drinks, and after a few Bob asked Bing to sing for us. Bing started singing with his pipe in his mouth, and without warning Bob reached over and took the pipe from Crosby, saying, 'You can't sing with that in your mouth!' "

FIVE U.S. PRESIDENTS

Daddy once told me that, over the years, five U.S. presidents had sought his advice on livestock production, agriculture, and economic development. My parents were friends and supporters of President Eisenhower and attended his inauguration. In June 1961, my mother noted in her journal that they had lunch with the Eisenhowers at Belmont before attending the Belmont Stakes. Later that year, she wrote that my father flew to San Antonio for a meeting with former President Eisenhower.

TWO PRINCESSES

Also in 1961, my parents greeted Maria Gabriella, the princess of Savoy, Princess Catherine de Croy, and Virginia Cohen. Princess Maria Gabriella was the daughter of King Humbert II of Italy. Princess Catherine was a descendant of Prince Benoit Azy, the creator of the Charolais breed of cattle. (Jean Pugibet of Mexico City kept a small, fine herd of Charolais at his home in Mexico City. The first bull of that breed to come to the United States arrived at King Ranch as a calf in the 1960s.) My mother wrote in her diary: "On Tuesday they attended a round up at the Crystal and ate lunch in camp. That evening they were driven to the coast where they met all of the Armstrongs. On Wednesday we took the girls to shop at King Ranch Saddle Shop. I taught them how to shoot a pistol and had lunch at the pool house where they had hamburgers."

Another dear friend was Mona Hind Holmes, a descendent of Kamehameha, the last king of Hawaii. She and my mother partnered in a small herd of Santa Gertrudis cattle on the big island of Hawaii. They got started by buying heifers at a 4-H sale in Texas; Daddy loaned them a King Ranch bull. Barbie Anthony, a family friend, saw how well Mona's cows were doing. She bought a few—then more—and went on to become the primary lady cattle breeder in the world.

Artists Peter and Henriette Wyeth Hurd, Tom and Sarah Lea, Louis Lundean, and other artist, writer, and photographer friends came to share ranch life.

A LIVING LABORATORY

For many years, King Ranch has been recognized as a living laboratory by top government and university educators, including geneticists, scientists, agronomists, and botanists. In cooperative arrangements with Grandfather Kleberg, my father, and King Ranch, they have traveled to the ranch to conduct research on problems related to water conservation, grass, livestock production, brush control, and diseases.

In the fall of 1953, Uncle Dick (Congressman Kleberg) and my father hosted an educational conference in honor of King Ranch's 100th birthday. The agenda recognized the contributions of animal sciences to the progress of King Ranch. It also focused on beef production in tropical climates around the world, because these regions offered the most promise for the production of beef for a growing population. Attending this conference were faculty from sixteen North American universities, Cambridge University, the University of São Paulo, and the University of Adelaide in Australia. Agricultural technicians and cattle breeders came from Argentina, Australia, Brazil, Colombia, Cuba, Great Britain, Venezuela, South Africa, and the United States. Ranchers, newsmen, and friends of the King Ranch also participated.

(preceding page)
65 Bing Crosby, Bob Kleberg Jr., Tom Armstrong (in poncho) hunting on King Ranch, 1960s

(following pages)
66 From left: Helen K. Kleberg, King Michael, Helen C. Kleberg, Bobby Shelton, Henrietta Larkin, Bob Kleberg Jr., 1948

67 Bob Kleberg Jr. and Mrs. Will Rogers, 1940s

68 Artist Peter Hurd at King Ranch, 1957

69 Artist Henrietta Wyeth Hurd with her painting *The Three Helens*, 1956. In painting (from left): Helen K. Alexander, Helen C. Alexander, and Helen C. Kleberg.

66

69

Children

Growing up at the King Ranch

Big adventures, lessons learned

The girls began helping their mothers at a young age. Their work included washing clothes in a large iron pot over an open fire, cooking beans, or making tortillas on a woodstove. They picked rocks out of beans and swept the dampened dirt floors in and around their homes. In those days, everything was ironed, including diapers, sheets, even underwear. Irons were heated on a woodstove. The girls also tended the most recent baby, washing the diapers and hanging them on a clothesline with the rest of the wash. Their work never seemed to end.

I have wonderful memories of growing up on the ranch and playing mostly with boys, who always seemed to have more free time than the girls. When we played baseball, they were very kind and let me pitch a lot. Sometimes we went over to the old Hitchcock Corral that Daddy had built for my mother to jump ponies. We played cops and robbers and broke little wooden swords over each other. There were never any tears about the pain or about breaking the swords, but there would be tears and fury over breaking the rules of the game, whatever they were.

We enjoyed shooting marbles or playing baseball after school. I was allowed to play down at the Kineños' houses as long as I was home by dark, a rule my mother insisted on. I will always remember standing on the high bridge that crossed Santa Gertrudis Creek, watching as Jesus Hinojosa carefully dropped a brick on the head of a duck, killing it. We were impressed with his patience and aim. Later he made a fine Marine.

Once, when the horse races were not in session, a group of us decided to imitate the grown-ups by having a race. We got buckets, grain, ropes, and halters and went down to the track. The barns didn't have electric lights, so there was a limit to how late we could stay. It took us quite a while to get everything done, since we had to put feed and water buckets up and put the horses away. By the time I got home, it was 9:30 and my mother was upset. "You know you're supposed to always be home by dark, or call!" she said. We invited the grown-ups to come watch. The winner of the race received a box of Whitman's Sampler chocolates. My cousin B. K. Johnson's mare Pimienta won.

CHRISTMAS

When I was a child, Christmas was always exciting. The commissary at Santa Gertrudis was the gathering place for Christmas Eve activities. Mana, other family, and my parents and I would be invited. We would stop by to greet the ranch employees and their families as they waited for Santa Claus. I always wanted to go up on the roof, but my mother said Santa's reindeer would

From left: Katherine Kleberg, Dick Kleberg Jr., Alice Kleberg (children of Congressman Richard Kleberg), and Helen K. Kleberg on her pony, Tordito

Kineño boys

get scared and fly off without him. I never got to see his reindeer or sleigh, but I knew they were up there. When Santa finally arrived, he handed out candy, fruit, and presents for the children. The women usually got something like a blanket; the men, a jacket; and teenagers, a pocketknife or perfume.

Afterward, everyone went over to the old Santa Gertrudis schoolhouse for a dance. The building looked enormous to me; I remember that the women wore long dresses and sat along the walls. The men, dressed in suits, would ask them to dance. Sometimes the ladies even changed clothes during the party. Mind you, there was no air-conditioning and it could be hot at Christmas time.

Before it was late, my parents and I would go home. Waiting for us were delicious tamales that had been prepared by the Silva family, who lived at Laureles. Tamales are a traditional holiday food at King Ranch, even today. There were never any presents or even a tree in our house on Christmas Eve, but Christmas morning, to my surprise, a beautifully decorated tree had appeared, with colorfully wrapped gifts under its branches. Mana came over from the big house to eat breakfast. After we opened our presents,

my parents telephoned my mother's family and other friends, offering Christmas wishes. We would go to Mana's for lunch. Many times we ate a wild turkey Daddy had shot on the way from Los Amigos Camp. In the afternoon we started for Los Amigos camp, often stopping at the Armstrong ranch on the way.

EDUCATION FOR ALL

My mother served on the Kleberg County School Board, representing the ranch's Santa Gertrudis School. She initiated a new concept in education for this region of Texas. It consisted of home economics, sewing, and cooking classes for the girls and carpentry and shop classes for the boys. Eventually, with my mother's prompting, these courses were made part of the curriculum in the Kingsville schools. She was later named president of the Board of Trustees for the Santa Gertrudis School District. .

Leroy Denman Jr. recalls, "Helen took great interest in education and would often talk to the teachers about how they ran the schools. She was a great teacher herself and often held contests to see which students spoke the best English. It was a great event when the pupils could perform before the 'Madama' at King Ranch's three schools—Laureles, Norias, and Santa Gertrudis."

My mother held contests with prizes for the nicest yards around the King Ranch employees' homes. She was also a deputy sheriff over the years, which gave her the ability to carry a weapon and make arrests. As far as I know, she never had to.

On the Range

Drought and dust, boom and bust

Ranch work

ROUNDUPS

Daddy loved working cattle horseback in roundups. Up before dawn, the cowboys were in place for the gather by daylight. The boss would have considered the prevailing wind, distance between waterings, and other variables. By 9:00 A.M., the herd was in place, "settling" and mothering up, while horses were changed and the men had a quick breakfast.

"Mr. Bob" and the local ranch foreman looked over the herd as they rode into its midst. They would remember not only which animals they wanted to cut out, but which calf belonged to which cow. First the cows no longer wanted were cut out with their calves; then old or injured stock and orphans; and finally the yearlings. Sometimes we took turns changing horses and going to lunch. At about 3:30 P.M. the roping and branding began.

I was not much of a roper, but Daddy and the others might ride three or four horses depending on whether there were 200 to 300 calves, and depending on their size and the temperature. Every effort was made to keep the daily branding to less than 300, especially when men were throwing calves all afternoon in the heat and dust. Working day after day, they would wear out.

After several days of roundup, or perhaps daily, the cut had to be shaped by category in the pens and shipped out by truck. In earlier days, before World War II, cattle that were cut out were driven to pens by the railroad. This demanding routine continued daily for months, until the last calf had been branded and released.

Kineños heating branding irons

Ed Durham's father was a Texas Ranger before working for Captain King. Ed and his son, Lavoyger, worked many a herd with Daddy. They had a great love and understanding of Norias. Ed used to say, "If you go with it, this country will reward you. If you fight it, you'll lose."

Lolo Treviño, a semi-retired fourth-generation Kineño, remembers Daddy at work:

When Mr. Bob came to the roundup, he always shook my hand. He would run his left hand over my horse's neck, ears, and mane, while asking, "How you been doin'? How's your brother, your father, your momma?" He knew them all. As he talked, he would go on petting the horse, looking at the brand and checking the tail for ticks or burrs.

He would work all day long with us and even sleep in camp. If he was on foot, he was helping you. If he was on horseback, he was helping you. Mr. Bob could do any job as well as any of us and would stay till the last calf was branded. He was proud that we were his people and his team. . . . I have said to people who visit King Ranch, we have always worked like a family, the workers and the owners.

Lieutenant General Marc Cisneros, United States Army, Retired, the former president of Texas A&M University-Kingsville recalls: "Bob Kleberg was a great leader among the cowboys on the ranch. He was raised with the people and was very knowledgeable of their culture. He spoke their language. He respected them and protected them because he knew he had their complete loyalty."

During the roundups the dust that filled the air was terrible. While the men worked, they often could not recognize each other because they were covered in so much dust. Everyone wore glasses and bandannas over their faces. Daddy suffered from hay fever, especially ragweed. He told me sometimes it was so bad that he would get up in the night and have my mother drive him to the coast. But he would say, "I have hay fever, not allergies!" He thought allergies were some kind of affectation, not a legitimate condition.

When my mother's health permitted it, she loved to go to roundups and would go flat out on a good cutting horse. Once when she was riding Venadita, a little mare, she ran broadside into a big bull. Daddy asked what she was thinking. "I thought he'd get out of my way," she said. She had no fear. Occasionally, she roped calves by their heels, dragging them to the fire where they were branded and vaccinated.

When my mother was at roundups, she covered her face with a chiffon scarf and wore glasses. A wide-brimmed cowboy hat shaded her from the sun's rays. Her hair was always tied up in a bandanna. Mary Lewis Kleberg remembers, "Helen was a beautiful horsewoman. She loved to work with the cowboys and get just as dusty as the rest of them."

DEPRESSION YEARS

After the stock market crash in 1929, Daddy faced one of his greatest challenges. Across the country, jobs were scarce, and food and money were short. Many banks were forced to close in what was referred to as a "bank holiday." My family's bank, however—which was organized in 1905 as an independent community bank serving the Kingsville area—never closed its doors throughout the Depression.

To make matters worse, rain stopped falling, and the sun turned millions of acres to dust. Thousands of thirsty and starving livestock died, and what had been the "Breadbasket of America" became the Dust Bowl. Since there was no money to buy beef, there was no market for cattle and thus no money to pay anyone. Gathering the Kineños together or speaking to them one on one, Daddy reassured them all. "You know we've got shelter, we've got milk, we've got meat. You can keep a garden, and we'll furnish you with rice, beans, sugar and coffee. If anyone is sick we'll see to it that you get medicine somehow, but there's no money to pay you. When conditions improve, we'll be able to pay you and fix your houses." They trusted Daddy and stayed.

During this period, my father needed some good Brahman bulls, so he wrote J. D. Hudgins of Hungerford, Texas, asking to purchase 100 bulls of Manso Brahman breeding. He said, "I can't pay you now, but will as soon as I can." Mr. Hudgins agreed. The ranch received the bulls and Hudgins was soon paid.

THE MESQUITER

Mesquite has been a constant threat to many Texas ranches, and King Ranch is no exception. The tree's thirsty roots spread rapidly, sapping moisture from grasses and reducing the available nutrition. During the Depression, Daddy offered many men the opportunity to work chopping mesquite. Many years earlier, Grandfather Kleberg had experimented with a brush-

Land clearing demonstration. Dr. John Hammond (left), Santa Gertrudis Auction, April 1959.

clearing machine that was quickly abandoned in favor of men with axes.

My father had a good understanding of mechanics and engineering and realized that hand labor was not practical, so he took an idea to R. G. LeTourneau, a dynamic businessman whose company designed and built the world's largest earth-moving machines. Daddy wanted LeTourneau to build a tractor powerful enough to clear brush in one operation—that is, to knock down trees in front while pulling a root plow behind. The machine he created, the Mesquiter, was an iron-wheeled tractor weighing more than 100 tons. It was assembled at King Ranch, but it was so enormous and heavy that it broke down frequently, never going more than two miles. Another impractical machine!

When Daddy heard that L. F. (Red) Wilkinson was at the Santa Gertrudis shop visiting his son, he asked Wilkinson to our home. When their conversation was over, Red was no longer a retired farmer and Holt Caterpillar tractor dealer; he was collaborating with my father on how to clear land by harnessing two D9 Caterpillar tractors together. The tractors pulled a great iron chain weighing thousands of pounds across the pasture to uproot the mesquite. Wilkinson devised a twenty-four-hour operation where three men worked successive shifts. He fine-tuned his tools and techniques and eventually cleared land elsewhere in Texas and Cuba, Venezuela, Australia, and other countries. Some retirement!

THE BUSH TELEGRAPH

To help Daddy keep in touch with employees at Santa Gertrudis, José Alegría, our family cook, served as his liaison. Each morning, José had coffee ready in the kitchen, and by 4:00 A.M. many men had arrived to have a cup and visit with him. Later, José would convey their concerns to my father. Daddy would say, "José, tell them to come by the house this evening." At the appointed hour Daddy would be on the porch to meet whoever needed him, to listen to their concerns and decide what to do. This type of communication stopped when more people got telephones and pickups.

Daddy sent for Adan Muñoz, already a cowboy on the ranch like his forebears, when he was twenty-one. Adan recalled, "Mr. Bob told me, 'I want you to look after me and mine and see what needs to be done. I never want to have to tell you what to do.' And he never did, but sometimes he told me personally what I should not do." Horses, guns, cars, equipment, and many people's needs were in Adan's care.

(preceding page)
78 Bob Kleberg Jr. directing at a roundup, circa 1942

(facing page)
79 Adan Muñoz, Bob's right-hand man

(following pages)
80 Moving cattle on King Ranch

81 Ed Durham with bloodhound, 1950s

82 Manuel Silva cutting at Laureles, circa 1940

83 Bob Kleberg Jr. (left) and the Laureles cowboys

84 Helenita cutting yearlings

85 Branding time at Laureles, 1941

86 Gathering herd for branding at Laureles, 1941

87 Branding at King Ranch, Norias

88 Kineño holding a calf, Laureles

89 Kineño grooming with cow chip, circa 1940

90 Chowtime at cow camp

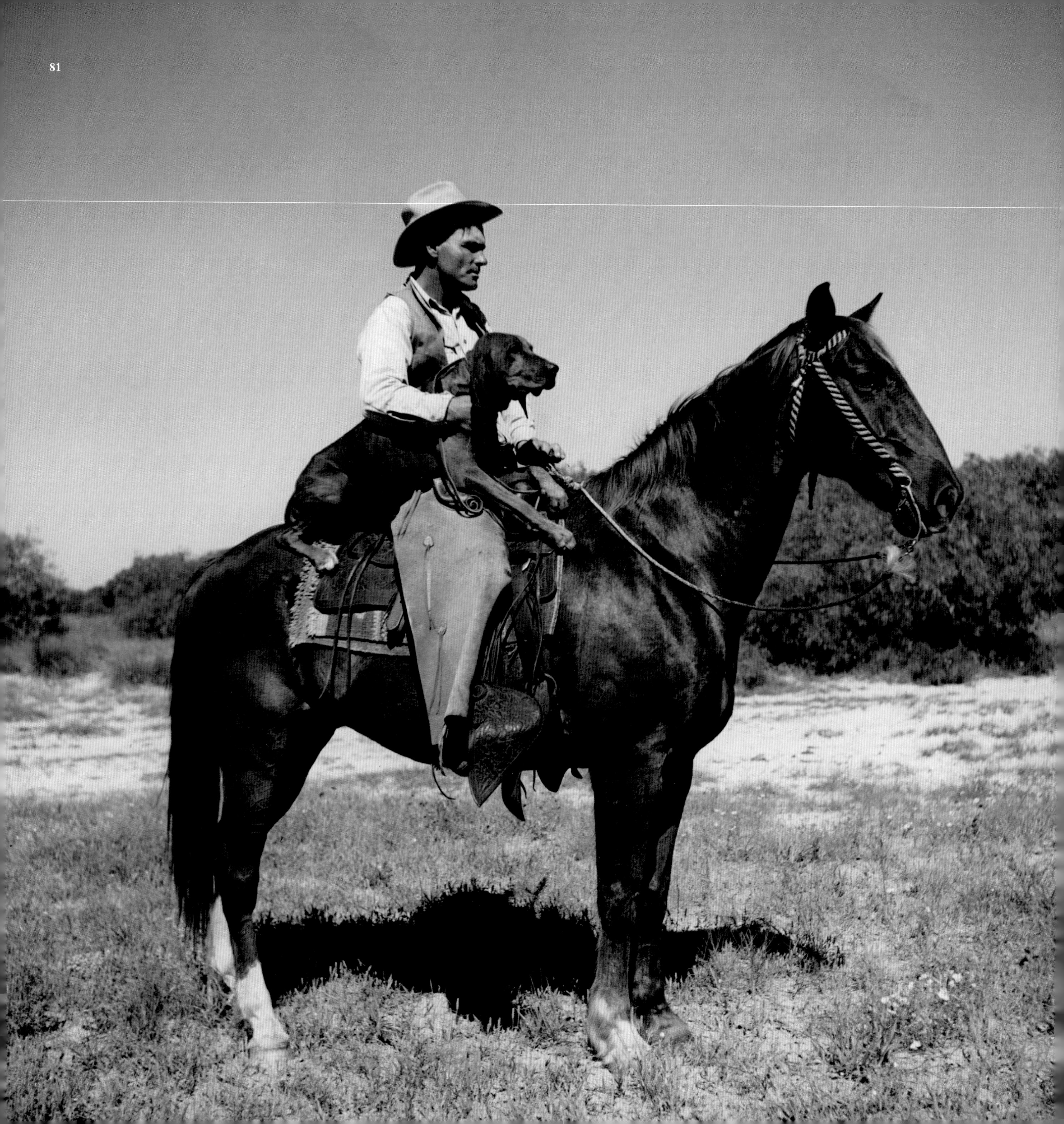

85

88

Helenita

"Raised . . . among horses, dogs and
all manner of animals"

Growing up to grown-up

I was born Helen King Kleberg on October 20, 1927, in San Antonio, and was promptly called Helenita. My parents taught me the importance of discipline, respect for others, and proper manners. At an early age, I learned to respect our land, water, and property, and everyone else's, too. My mother insisted that whenever I borrowed anything, I should return it in as good condition as I received it or better.

A 1930 article quoted my mother: "I have a little girl three years old, named Helen King Kleberg, who is being raised according to the customs of the country among horses, dogs and all manner of animals. I have taught her one verse of "Onward Christian Soldiers," which she sings with great zest. She can also discern with ease the difference between a coyote track and a bobcat track in the sand."[44]

My mother was not fond of all my pets, especially my deer, which nipped off the rosebuds she had worked so diligently to grow. Occasionally, the deer joined my pet calf in butting the grapefruit from the trees that grew around our house at Santa Gertrudis.

I always respected my parents, but at times I was a trying child. They chose Lucía Gonzalez to be my loving nurse. Once, when Lucía was trying to lead me by the hand from Mana's house to ours for lunch, I stomped her foot with my cowboy boot. When we got home, Daddy asked Lucía why she was limping. And when he heard what I had done, he sat me down and gave me a good lecture about respecting the rights of others. Then he gave me a spanking, the only one I remember getting from him.

My parents kept loaded pistols in their holsters, strapped to the headboard of their bed. When I was around four, my father took me into their bedroom, pointed at the ceiling, and said, "You see those little dents? They were caused by 'unloaded guns.' Just to be sure there's no mistake, all of my guns are loaded at all times. Don't forget that, and don't touch them." I never did.

PONIES

When I was four, Mrs. McFaddin of Victoria, a friend of my parents, gave me a pony named Tordito. He was a wonderful pony with a little star on his face. He probably would have been black if the sun hadn't turned him so brown. He was my racehorse, my cow horse, and my pet. I used to go down to the racetrack to watch the activities. Poor Tordito put up with all the grooming that the racehorses got. I remember my mother giving me a sofa cover to use as a sheet for him. He had to have his feet picked out and his teeth brushed, and he endured baths with a little bit of alcohol in the water just like the racehorses.

When I was seven, just before the annual Christmas party, I received a wonderful surprise. Daddy's nephew, Tom East, arrived leading a beautiful yellow-and-white pony. I named him Pinto. At that time, we had a little paddock with a white board fence in front of our house where I kept Tordito, so we put Pinto in with him. That was one of the nicest Christmas gifts I had ever received. The following year, I was really amazed—I was given a saddle that Santa Claus actually brought down the chimney.

Bob Kleberg Jr. and family, 1930s

THE CALVERT SYSTEM

When I was almost six, my mother introduced me to the Calvert System. I still recall the first words I learned to read and write: "I see a—." Then I would draw a picture and write down a word such as "ball," "dog," or "tree." My parents took me everywhere, whether it was to roundups on the ranch or hotels in New York. Almost every day, wherever we were, I had school with my mother. Occasionally she might let me have a day off to go to a roundup. When we camped out in the winter at Norias, we worked on my lessons while Daddy and the others gathered the cattle. Afterward, my mother and I joined the men. My classes never lasted more than three hours a day, usually in the morning. Here's a typical week, recorded in my mother's journal:

> February 7, 1935. School for Helen.
>
> February 9. School for Helen.
>
> February 10. Go to field trial early. This is the day of running of state championship. Sam Cheshire won first in shooting dog class with Caesar's Jack. Cold and rainy as the dickens.
>
> February 11. Woke up with headache and couldn't go out to see Bob handle his dog Dixie. Helen caught cold yesterday. She got another perfect report today from Calvert School.

NOT SO FEARLESS

I believed my mother was fearless. She once took a loaded gun, pointed straight at her, out of a drunk man's hand without showing any emotion. I didn't think she was afraid of anything. Then one day a terrifying scream came from her bedroom. I rushed in, and there she was, on top of the bed, trying to climb the bedpost. I couldn't believe it. She frantically shouted for our cook, José, to help her. In the gun cabinet drawer were some baby mice. When she spotted them she was overcome. How could someone so brave and authoritative be so afraid of such tiny creatures? This was the only time I ever saw my mother, who was always so strong and determined, show even a hint of fear.

FOXCROFT

My mother taught me the last year of the Calvert System with the help of a math tutor. In the fall of 1940 I had a taste of overcrowding in the public schools, in Kingsville with 56 students in my classroom. The following fall, I entered Foxcroft, a girls' boarding school in the Virginia countryside, four miles from Middleburg. When I arrived, many of the girls thought Texas was home to wild Indians. New York girls thought that "way down South" meant Baltimore and that Pittsburgh was "way out West." Then there was California, "out on an ocean somewhere." Many of them also thought the Pilgrims were the first people to come to America. They had no idea that San Antonio had missions and commerce before the Pilgrims arrived at Plymouth Rock.

For the next four years, I studied English, French, Latin, algebra, geometry, history, biology, and my favorite, creative art. I found Foxcroft pretty hard, but I soon learned to concentrate when I really needed to. The second year, Daddy sent me a King Ranch mare by Old Sorrel, out of a Thoroughbred mare; for a year, I averaged falling off her once a week. She would lower her shoulder and drop me or shy or rear suddenly. But she and I learned to fox hunt together, which was the closest thing in the East to rounding up cattle in the brush.

PEARL HARBOR

The afternoon of December 7, 1941, was gloomy and overcast. We girls were sitting around with the radio on in the background. When the announcer broke in, we didn't pay much attention until we heard him say that Pearl Harbor had been bombed. A classmate, Anne Matheson, grew alarmed. Her California family had interests in Hawaii, and she was unable to reach her parents on the telephone. It was frightening for all of us, but

Helen C. Kleberg taking nose drops, late 1920s

Helenita and B. K. Johnson
at Belmont Track, 1946

we rallied around her. The surprise attack that morning nearly destroyed our Pacific Fleet. America declared war on Japan, and soon long lines of young men volunteered or were drafted to serve our country. I did not know then that Uncle Colin, a naval captain, was stationed at Pearl Harbor with his family.

It's hard for people today to realize what a fear of invasion we had at that time. We were afraid the Germans would step out of their submarines onto the coast or the Japanese would land on our western shores. When the Kineños were working cattle at Laureles, a dud bomb scattered the herd that Dick Kleberg Jr. was moving. We thought it was the Germans.

At King Ranch keeping up with the work became increasingly difficult. Charlie Burwell, manager of the Laureles division, went to the local draft board and pleaded, "Please leave me an able-bodied cowboy on this ranch!" The board said the only solution was to train the younger employees and use the older ones. "We have some that are so old that they can't lift the younger ones into the saddle," Charlie said. "We need some able-bodied men!" His urgent request was to no avail. My mother noted in her journal on April 13, 1943: "We are losing workmen all the time to the Naval Base. We still have some cowboys, but our labor is practically nil."

OIL EXPLORATION

America was at war and needed oil. Humble Oil Company soon stepped up its exploration on King Ranch and began pumping oil out of the ground. I remember my father's response to this: "I had hoped this would not happen," he said. "Everything will change, and ranching will no longer be the life we have known it to be." He was right. As roads to aid the oil development were built, trucks and trailers replaced horseback cowboys and wagons, changing ranching as much as the arrival of the railroads had in earlier times.

THE WAR EFFORT

Soon after the attack on Pearl Harbor, my mother completed several Red Cross courses. She became

Helenita in Fiesta gown, San Antonio, 1940

very active in the Red Cross, serving as a director of the Volunteer Service Committee and working with the Volunteer Special Services, which organized volunteer committees and reported their activities to the national-area headquarters in St. Louis. She also organized the Camp-Hospital Council in South Texas and devoted a great deal of time to the United Services Organization. Together, my parents hosted many active-duty military personnel at the ranch.

In addition to these civic activities, my mother worked cattle horseback with Daddy and organized meals for guests, even though most materials were rationed and in short supply. When the first signs of war appeared, my mother said there were two items she could not do without—toilet paper and soap. She stocked up on toilet paper and decided to make lye soap in an old iron kettle over an open fire. Big vats of lye soap were cut into white blocks and stashed in the commissary. Sometime later my mother received a crate of apples from a guest and directed that the iron kettle be used again, this time to make apple butter. Unfortunately, there was no way anyone could swallow that stuff. No one had told her that once you boil lye in an iron pot, you can never use it to cook anything else.

BUCK AND DOE RUN VALLEY FARMS

In 1946, Daddy decided to purchase some property in Chester County, Pennsylvania. It was his first property venture outside of South Texas. My mother enjoyed this beautiful country, which reminded her of Virginia, where she had grown up. Daddy believed this property could be a premium fattening area for cattle in the northeastern part of the United States. He hired a young man, Burnett Wilson, to be the general manager. My parents spent a lot of time at Buck and Doe. It was also my home when my children were young.

In later years, when my parents came to visit, they loved to picnic with us at the twin bridges. My mother occasionally had Sunday lunch for racing and other friends, with roast beef or Virginia ham, a casserole of eggs poached in tomatoes, and other buffet items. William DuPont and the Plunket Stewarts were often guests. We went to visit Andy Wyeth when he and his wife, Betsy, and their young sons still lived in the "schoolhouse," before he was famous.

MY MOTHER'S ILLNESS

I was always close to my parents. When I went off to Foxcroft, and later to Vassar College, I telephoned often and wrote many letters. Each summer and Christmas, I returned home to be with them. It wasn't until the summer of 1947 that I learned my mother had been suffering from a serious illness. I decided I was needed at home and did not return to Vassar. I knew my mother was occasionally in bed with terrible migraines, but she never made a fuss or talked about it. I thought that when Daddy asked her not to work so hard, he just wanted her undivided attention. He did, of course, but he was also trying to protect her.

Unbeknownst to me, when I was about six months old my mother was diagnosed with pulmonary tuberculosis. Within a few months her condition worsened. With Daddy at her side, she entered Union Memorial Hospital in Baltimore and was told that the disease plaguing her was extremely dangerous; she would have to change her environment and physical activities immediately.

My mother continually monitored her activity level to minimize stress. Toward the end of 1941, she wrote Dr. Roy Adams of Washington, D.C.: "I have been leading a very sedentary life of which even you would approve, going to bed early at night, getting up late in the morning, with a nap after lunch. I have gained so many pounds due to my good appetite that I feel now that I shall have to cut down and watch my calories; however, I shall keep on with the milk. . . . I won't say that I feel as good as new, because I cannot go as far as I could before I was ill, but more than any-thing I am being very careful not to force myself beyond my strength, which increases day to day."

Though it was rare, she occasionally received a good report. Toward the end of 1946, Dr. Walter Baetjer advised that, despite some signs of the disease in her right lung and an attack she had suffered the previous winter, my mother should consider herself healthy: "With the obvious healing that has gone on, it can only mean that your underlying resistance is fine and that you have gotten by without having to be made an invalid. On the other hand, I think we must always remember that this could come back." Throughout the years, my mother took various medications, was constantly monitored, and was often forced to stay indoors and rest. But it seemed that no matter how closely she followed her doctor's guidelines, her condition was never stable.

In November 1947, she received a warning from Dr. Baetjer: "I frankly don't like the recurrence of the little bit of fever that you had. . . . I feel you are living over a volcano and that you must try to be absolutely careful this winter and see that nothing gets started."

DUCHESS OF KINGSVILLE

On April 22, 1947, my mother wrote in her diary, "Helenita's coming out party." I had come home from Vassar to be introduced to South Texas society by my parents during Fiesta, a major celebration in San Antonio similar to New Orleans' Mardi Gras. I wore a white marquisette gown with graceful green leaf motifs, appliquéd on a full skirt that cascaded from a narrow green belt. I had a tight-fitting bodice in an off-the-shoulder design, with soft folds of the material caught with a small green bow. With a white orchid in my hair, I carried a colonial bouquet of gardenias and sweetheart roses, a gift from Granny Campbell. I was the Duchess of Kingsville in the Coronation Court of the Battle of Flowers Fiesta, commemorating the Battle of San Jacinto. What fun!

From left: Harry Weiss, president of Humble Oil, Bob Kleberg Jr., and Helenita hunting, circa 1945

Helen K. (Kleberg) Alexander and Dr. Deaver Alexander, circa 1950

Bob Kleberg Jr. and Helen K. Kleberg (Groves) at Armstrong Ranch's Washington's Birthday cattle sale, late 1960s

GIANT

The warnings and restrictions from Dr. Baetjer frustrated my mother. To make matters worse, she came down with a sore throat, a cough, and a fever. It was the middle of summer 1947. The constant confinement, lack of physical activity, and depressing medical reports were too much. Against all medical advice, and the pleas of Daddy and me, my mother went on a two-mile walk in the hottest part of the day.

It turned out that this was the day Edna Ferber, the author of *Cimarron* and *Showboat*, was to join us for lunch. She arrived while Mother was out. Betty Stevens, a friend of mine from New Orleans, was visiting. After Mother returned from her walk, Daddy tried to calm her and get her into bed while I arranged the meal.

Soon after we sat down, Ms. Ferber told my father she was going to write a novel based on him, my mother, and King Ranch. After listening patiently, Daddy said that sometime in the future there would be an accurate history written which she and others could reference, but he did not have the time at present to devote to it. Furthermore, he added, he did not want an inaccurate book written. Ms. Ferber insisted that she would write the book anyway and became rude. Daddy turned to me and said, "Helenita, please call for Ms. Ferber's driver. He's in the kitchen. She wants to leave now and won't be coming back."

Betty and I were silent. I know we hadn't had our coffee when Daddy took Ms. Ferber's arm and escorted her to the door. She never returned. Sure enough, though, a few years later her book *Giant* became a bestseller. It was made into a movie, starring Rock Hudson, Elizabeth Taylor, and James Dean.

A LONG WINTER

In July 1948, we took my mother to Baltimore to evaluate her tuberculosis at Union Memorial Hospital. After a short stay, we went to Buck and Doe Run Valley Farms in Pennsylvania. The weeks that followed were monotonous, as my mother was again forced to stay in bed to rest. In August, Daddy suggested I take a few days off to go to Saratoga, New York, for a change of pace. There I saw Deaver Alexander, a resident doctor in New York City. I had met him earlier at a party in Pennsylvania. Deaver visited me at Buck and Doe when he could, but most of my time was spent looking after my mother.

On October 12, 1948, my mother began having a lung hemorrhage. I put a wet cloth over her head, held her in my arms, and tried to help her breathe. I called Deaver, who said Mother needed to get to the University of Pennsylvania Hospital without delay. She was taken by ambulance to the hospital and placed in an oxygen tent. That winter was long and lonely for all. Finally, after a five-month stay, my mother returned with Daddy to King Ranch. Then they made plans for a big event.

A WEDDING

After dating for some time, Dr. John Deaver Alexander and I were married on April 16, 1949. Deaver was the son of Mrs. Emory Graham Alexander and the late Dr. Alexander of Philadelphia. He was a graduate of Princeton University and the University of Pennsylvania Medical School. A member of the St. Anthony Club, the White Marsh Hunt Club, the Racquet Club of Philadelphia, and the Princeton Club of New York, he was the grandson of the late Dr. and Mrs. John B. Deaver of Philadelphia.

Our wedding was held in the Church of the Epiphany in Kingsville, at twilight during the Easter season. Our reception was at the big house at Santa Gertrudis, where we greeted approximately 2,000 guests. Toni Frissell was there and took many photographs. My mother wanted me to have a big wedding since hers was so small. It was superb. After the reception, Deaver and I went to Norias and on to Mexico City for our honeymoon. My mother wrote in her diary, "Back to bed for a month."

SETBACK AND RECOVERY

Toward the end of 1949, my mother suffered another setback. She hadn't improved by January, so Daddy took her to Baltimore, where she was hospitalized for several months. On Easter Sunday, she received a special treat; she was permitted to leave the hospital with my father to attend Easter services. Afterward, they strolled around the corner and, as my mother wrote, "We had lunch in the dining room I love!"

My mother was released after nearly four months, and my parents flew back to Kingsville. The next day she was up for lunch and out with Daddy to watch the racehorses being led to the train station for their trip to the track at Belmont, New York.

During the early part of 1951, my mother's migraines grew worse. She was losing her strength, and it was becoming more difficult for her to breathe and sleep. Shortly after being admitted to the Presbyterian Hospital in New York City, she wrote in her journal:

> Upper right lobe badly diseased—the bronchi also involved and not enough left to salvage. I have a 50-50 chance of returning to activity, after perhaps 2 years of bed rest, a 95-5 chance. If they take out the upper right lobe—operation by Dr. Berry, it will involve roughly 6 months bed rest followed by 6 months great care semi-active, I suppose. It is a unanimous opinion of the doctors that an operation is feasible and the better course. They get the go sign from me!

The surgery was a great success, and on April 15 my mother was released. My parents drove to Buck and Doe, where she rested and recovered.

Several years after my mother underwent surgery, she was much stronger and resumed many of her physical activities. Best of all, she was not restricted to bed and was able to travel with Daddy, whether it was to attend the Kentucky Derby, meet the King and Queen of England, attend the running of the Triple Crown, or conduct business in Australia, Cuba, Argentina, or some other country.

LA ESCONDIDA

My mother loved hunting and fishing and took advantage of opportunities to do both all over the world. Twice at Norias she shot two wild turkeys in the neck with one bullet as they crossed one behind the other. In early February 1961, she wrote in her diary: "Fair and warm today, Bob is working at San Tomás. I went to Escondida to fish alone. The water is clear and beautiful, no turtles, many fish—The monster got away!" She sketched a turtle trap she wanted to have built.

After her death, on June 12, 1963, of an incurable brain tumor, she was buried near her favorite fishing spot, La Escondida, at Norias, which Daddy had built for her. After Daddy's death on October 13, 1974, he was buried beside her. At the end of each day, dusk blankets the oaks that stand over my parents' graves. The birds fly overhead, and bass glide through the waters of the tiny lake. Whitetail deer, turkey, quail, javelina, and other wildlife make their way to the water's edge to quench their thirst.

92

93

95

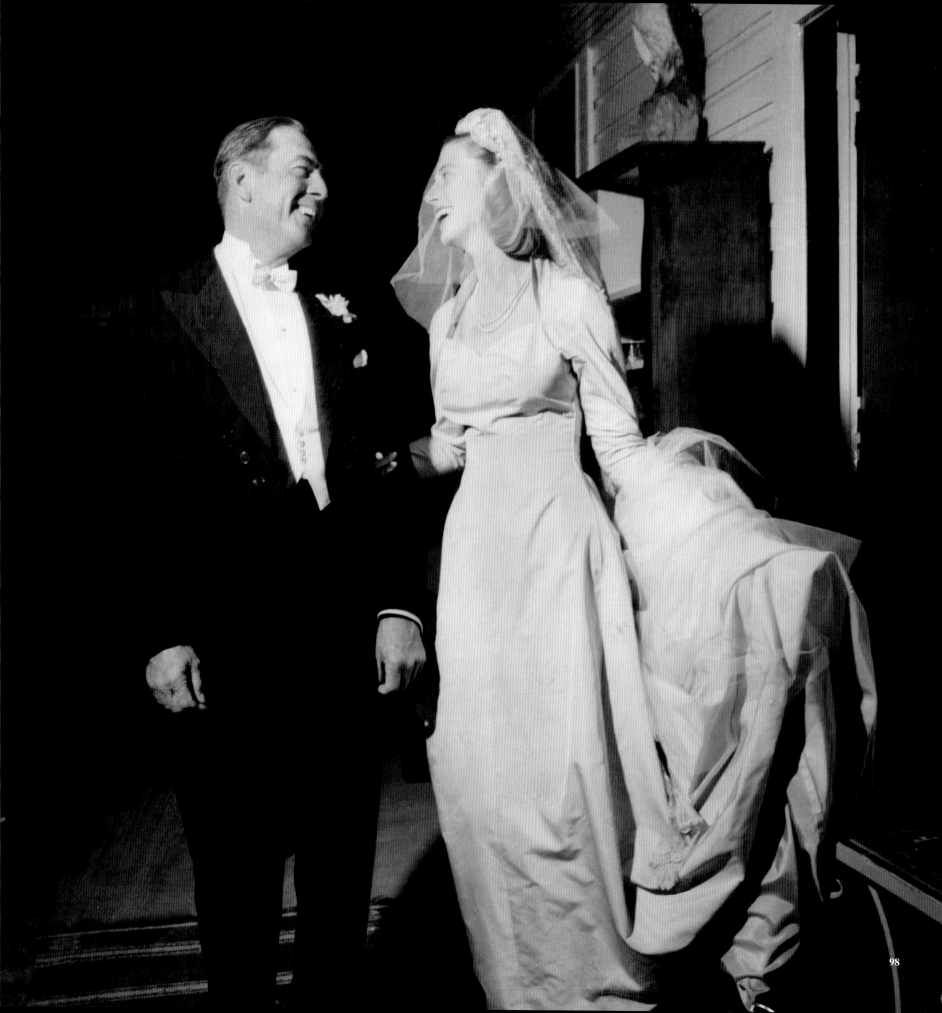

100

Resources in a Harsh Land

Water, water, water — precious resource — and food, glorious food

ARTESIAN WELLS

Dry conditions are the norm in South Texas. They shape the landscape and the lives of the inhabitants. One of Grandfather Kleberg's favorite sayings was "Civilization follows transportation." Grandfather's priority was finding a reliable source of water. Cisterns, dug wells, and tanks were useful, but they weren't dependable in long droughts. No trains could cross the Wild Horse Desert without a constant water source, nor could there be settlements.

On June 6, 1899, Grandfather and Mrs. King were photographed beside the first artesian well on King land. Located about two miles north of Santa Gertrudis headquarters, it was 532 feet deep. Grandfather said, "The men wondered why I cried when we finally saw what we had been praying for. But I knew that once a definite source of water was available I could induce railroad construction, which in turn would lead to the development of South Texas."[45]

For years Grandfather researched how to reduce the devastating effects of the climate. In Nebraska he found a well-drilling machine and a driller—Tom Leary and the Dempster Mill Manufacturing Company. He persuaded Leary to bring his rig to Santa Gertrudis and engaged another driller from the Texas Hill Country to work with him. Leary and his crew drilled eight wells, with water rushing out of the ground at 20 to 400 gallons a minute. The May 19, 1904, *Texas Stockman* reported, "One has but to see the green fields of alfalfa, sugar beets, and mangels

Robert J. Kleberg Sr. at first artesian well, June 6, 1899

flourishing under manager Kleberg's irrigation system, or glance at the great ricks of sorghum hay, to appreciate the fact that the truck gardener and the farmer will soon have possession of broad acres that have for generations served only as a cattle range."[46]

Grandfather Kleberg had accompanied Captain King on the initial celebratory trip when the railroad King had invested in was finished from Corpus Christi to Brownsville. Now that water-guzzling steam engines could be supplied, Grandfather again met with family friend and railroad promoter Uriah Lott. One day when Mr. Lott was expected for lunch, Mana admonished her children to take no notice of his nose, which was quite large and red. Of course, you know they embarrassed her as they choked on their laughter.

CONSERVATION

Daddy continued Grandfather's work to find ways to supplement the area's scarce water supply. He had lived with water shortages since his childhood, and he was well aware of the critical role water played in ranch life. During the drought of the 1930s, while he was general manager of Mrs. King's estate, he initiated a joint research effort between King Ranch and the federal government to explore water and soil conservation strategies.

This project, at the time the most extensive of its kind in the country, focused on the construction of dams and contours for pasture and field improvement, along with the eradication of mesquite trees and brush. Five large water holes and twelve earthen dams, ranging in length from several hundred feet to 8,400 feet, were constructed. The *South Texan* reported: "Bob

Kleberg emphasized the value of careful engineering work on range conservation projects if permanent benefits are to be enjoyed. . . . He explained that the engineers put in as much work on study of the project as the state or federal highway departments would do in planning a new highway."[47]

Towering windmills, driven by nearly constant winds, pumped cool water from below the earth's surface into large concrete troughs my father had designed. They were thirty feet in diameter and two feet deep, with a concrete footer around the outside. The footer gave calves a firm foothold so they could reach the water to drink. Inside these tanks were half-moon concrete steps to help calves, pigs, and other livestock that might fall in scramble to safety. Daddy also made sure there was some overflow for thirsty wildlife.

In the 1950s, one of the worst droughts of the century settled in, extending across the central United States from North Dakota into Mexico. At King Ranch, valuable grasses that once fed the livestock dried up. Dust drifted through fences, piling up like snow. It was so bad that we closed the house by 11:00 A.M. You had to dust your house every day, and even then, as you prepared to write a letter, the paper was covered with grit. Working the roundups was especially difficult. As each day passed, the need for moisture grew more critical. We had no water. In desperation, Daddy made a call. On October 19, 1950, my mother wrote in her diary, "Bob made contact with a rainmaker; he will start within 30 days."

This was not the first time a rainmaker had been called to King Ranch. Grandfather Kleberg brought in a group of rainmakers in 1892. These experimenters bombed the skies with explosive balloons and artillery in hopes of making it rain. Although heavy rain occurred, few scientists would attribute it to the explosions. In the next fifty years, scientific advances, including seeding the clouds with silver iodide or dry ice, made the rainmaking procedure more "promising"!

It's not clear if the efforts Daddy commissioned in 1950 worked, but he certainly wasn't alone in using this technology. There were so many demands by ranchers and farmers to modify the weather during this drought and in the years that followed that the state legislature passed a law controlling cloud-seeding operations.

Daddy's inventive mind was always looking for scientific solutions, rainmaking included. He explored another concept during the drought. In an effort to prevent water in the tanks from evaporating, he and my husband, Deaver, met with engineers at DuPont to discuss floating ping-pong-size plastic balls on the surface. As far as I know, nothing came of that idea.

As the drought continued, Daddy worked closely with the Texas and Southwestern Cattle Raisers Association and the Southwest Research Institute exploring means of conserving water. In an April 16, 1952, letter to J. M. Crews, chairman of the association's Water Resource Committee, my father told of research under way at the ranch: "We are putting down our first big well to the artesian sand, with the idea of putting water back into some of our water sands from surface lakes. Indications are that we can safely put this water back and by doing so we can raise the present static level. In plain language, it would be like putting water in a bottle where it would be less subject to evaporation."

CULVERTS AND DIKES

Throughout the world, wherever King Ranch purchased property, water and its proper use were foremost in Daddy's plans. When he first flew over northwestern Australia, he said, "All this country needs is water!" There was plenty of grass, but the wells were too far apart for the cattle to reach while grazing. When King Ranch expanded into Australia, he had water wells drilled and roads and dams constructed.

In Venezuela, at the King Ranch property El Cedral, lack of water wasn't the problem—quite the opposite. Floodwaters covered the land during certain seasons, making grazing impossible. Again, Daddy had a plan. Gustavo de los Reyes, my father's Cuban friend and associate in Venezuela, explained Daddy's idea to move millions of gallons of water from one area to another, using gravity: "The objective was to hold the floodwaters in a module and, through sedimentation, to capture the rich topsoil. Bob had culverts placed about one meter above the ground so that we were able to catch the deposited soil. The overflow water ran off. Bulldozers moved the trapped topsoil into dikes, converting this flood plain into a wonderful grass-growing region."

Gustavo recalled that the Venezuelan government wanted the ranch to use these dikes to haul water, but their purpose was to hold water for the dry season and to capture topsoil: "Once the dikes were completed, our cattle could eat and sleep on dry ground. Bob Kleberg knew what most people did not, that a well-managed pasture conserves the fertility of the soil and prevents erosion much more efficiently than a forest. El Cedral became the most productive venture of all the enterprises of King Ranch."

(preceding page)
101 Bob Kleberg Jr. with Laureles cowboys at water trough

(facing page)
102 Windmills pump water into concrete troughs for livestock

(following pages)
103 Cattle drinking at a 30-foot-diameter water trough with concrete footing, circa 1942

104 Cattle watering

105 Bob Kleberg Jr. washing up, circa 1940

106 Cowboys moving cattle to water, 1940s

107 Thirsty cowboy, 1940s

108 Kineños taking a break

109 Settling the dust at Telephone Pens, Laureles, circa 1940

Grand hospitality

My family, Santa Gertrudis, and King Ranch were known around the world for hospitality. Their social and business functions ranged from camp lunches to seated dinners in my parents' home and the big house. From the ranch's earliest days until the development of accessible towns with hotels and restaurants, invited guests, family, business associates, and strangers passing through King Ranch ate and rested. In 1881, during his first visit with Captain King, my grandfather Kleberg reported back to his family about the elaborate feast he enjoyed: "At the ranch a fine dinner awaited our arrival—Captain King has a regular French cook—and the table was loaded with good things to eat and drink; he lives like a prince and treats his friends to the best he has." Henrietta King, my great-grandmother, was a wonderful hostess and loved company. In winter she sometimes had barrels of oysters brought to Santa Gertrudis from Corpus Christi. In the shade behind the kitchen, the oysters were fattened on cornmeal. Later they were fried and enjoyed by friends and family.

In March 1931, the Texas and Southwestern Cattle Raisers Association held its convention in Corpus Christi. On the agenda was a tour of King Ranch. According to the meeting minutes, "At the invitation of the Kleberg Brothers, we saw hospitality given there, the like of which we had never seen before. I have reference to a certain breakfast. . . . They had four or five kinds of meat, three kinds of breakfast food, and two kinds of fruit, and they topped that off, for fear that we might not have had enough, by having waffles."[48]

Grandfather Kleberg was a great family man and generally sat down to three huge meals a day. For lunch the kitchen usually served soup, chicken, or fish, along with two or three vegetables, followed by desert. At night there was often dark meat such as venison, beef, lamb, or possibly duck, and occasionally quail and dove. Daddy told me that when he was a little boy, he and his brother would shoot sparrows and bring them to the cook, who would prepare sparrows en brochette.

KLEBERG COOKS

Willie Flores, Uncle Caesar's cook, was once sent to my mother to cook. He arrived in Kingsville on the morning train, but he went back to Norias that evening after making a lemon pie. It turned out that my mother didn't like lemon pie, and they simply didn't hit it off. He was a great cook with Uncle Caesar at Norias, but later, when the new headquarters was built, he blew up two gas stoves in rapid succession. It was just too dangerous for everyone, so my mother said he would have to cook outside. He was an excellent camp cook, and one of his great meals was to prepare everything from a calf, lamb, or goat, along with beans and rice. He could make wonderful camp bread, cornbread, and biscuits in the camp dutch ovens. A special dish was sweet potatoes cooked with orange wedges and molasses.

José Alegría, a former bronc-riding Kineño, was our wonderful cook. He wore a white starched chef's hat and uniform. One of his habits was to keep the salt on the top shelf of the cabinet. Each time he needed it, he would pull out the stepladder, climb up to retrieve the salt, use it, and climb up again to put it away. Then he would put the stepladder back. This ritual was repeated many times, nearly driving my mother mad.

Luís Prado, cook for Alice King Kleberg (Mana), 1942

José Alegría, cook for Bob Kleberg Jr. family, 1940

José prepared marvelous meals without ever measuring anything. He fixed excellent steak, roast beef, and lamb and baked a wonderful yellow layer cake. However, he had a dangerous habit of stoking too much mesquite wood in the iron cook stove. The intense heat would burn holes in the metal stove. My mother had to replace the stove every two years or risk a fire.

One day, she called José into the living room. "José," she said, "we're paying an exorbitant amount for food in this house. What's going on?"

"Well, Señora, don't you remember? Every day you have me prepare enough to feed the Mexican generals a good lunch. We have to order a lot of extra food, and then they don't come." He was referring to the military men who had said they wanted to buy horses for the Mexican army.

"We'll just stop preparing for the generals since we haven't heard from them," my mother said. That's the day the generals arrived. Lunch was prepared in haste!

One time a cattle buyer was lunching at our house. Deep in conversation with my father, he took his cue from others at the table, putting his finger bowl to the left of his dessert plate. When he spooned the floating island dessert into his mouth, the crocheted doily Granny had made went with it. We all held our breath. He swallowed it all!

Much of my parents' social life was business-related. They seldom had the luxury of dining alone. Indeed, on February 29, 1948, my mother recorded a rare event: "6 p.m. Dinner with Bob! Just us!"

Daddy was no vegetarian; he loved meat. During my childhood, we would often have a lunch that might include cold meat, such as sliced roast beef, sliced chicken, and ham, along with cheese and a potato or vegetable salad. Occasionally we had fish, which Daddy liked fried, with lemon and ketchup. We didn't eat salami or hot dogs. Later, when my parents were having guests from all over the world, there were some elaborate picnics organized out of the Norias kitchen to be taken into the fields, particularly during hunting season.

My mother liked to have soup first when we had company; if it wasn't soup, the first course might be sliced tomato broiled on toast. She was fond of saying, "You can cut back on many things, but always eat well. Fresh, simple food is best." She made a wonderful apple pie using brown sugar, butter, a little lemon juice, and a teaspoon of bourbon. The only time she went in to the kitchen was when José couldn't be there. I didn't want her to cook. I promise you, she used every single pot we had. She would turn out an excellent meal, but then she would say, "I've cooked, so someone else will have to clean up."

CAMPBELL TRADITIONS

I remember visiting my mother's parents, Granny and Grandpa Campbell, at Windsor and at Locust Hill Farm. Grandpa had been to Paris, and while he was there he learned to make a special salad dressing. In the evenings, he loved to mix this with the salad while we were seated around the table. He also had a routine of preparing Welsh rarebit on Sunday evenings.

Right after Thanksgiving at Locust Hill Farm, Granny Campbell would participate in one of her favorite activities. She, Aunt Elizabeth, Uncle Burdette, and other family members would butcher a hog. Working as a team, they put up hams, bacon, roasts, and ground and stuffed sausage. This family tradition stretched back to Granny's childhood and included many delicious recipes. Aunt Elizabeth learned well and continued the custom. My mother tried but without the same success. With all our modern conveniences, this is no longer a family ritual.

Thoroughbreds

The best! Winners of "the Derby," Preakness,
Belmont Stakes—and a Triple Crown

The sport of Kings

My father's understanding of genetics guided him in the development of the Santa Gertrudis breed. He then applied this interest to a new venture. During the 1930s, with encouragement from my mother, who loved Thoroughbreds, Daddy took King Ranch into the complex business of breeding and racing these horses.

As Daddy tells it, he heard of a good Quarter running mare on the John Dial ranch near Goliad, so he drove up to have a look. The mare, which was fifteen years old, was in good condition and still showed remarkably fine conformation. He decided to buy her and breed her in order to bring more speed to the ranch's horses. At the time he was interested in improving the cow horses, not horseracing.

His personal account gives us a valuable glimpse into his first work with Thoroughbreds:

> After I had seen the Quarter mare, [John Dial] insisted on showing me his Thoroughbreds, which he had also been breeding for many years—and especially Chicaro. Chicaro really was the most beautiful Thoroughbred horse I had ever seen up to that time, and I have seen few better or more perfect individuals since. John called my attention to his wonderful conformation and to the fact that his gaskin muscles in length size and strength were even better than on any Quarter Horse I had ever seen. John was continually expressing himself somewhat as follows: "You can't win races with loping horses," and also the old saying, "The first thing in a horse's life is speed."

Daddy liked everything he saw about Chicaro and decided he should go to Kentucky to see how such a tremendous Thoroughbred had been produced. He called my mother from the office one morning and asked if she could be ready to go in a couple of hours. She answered, "I could get ready to go to Europe in two hours!"

My parents set out in the car that day for Kentucky. Daddy drove until he became sleepy and Mother took over. By the time he awoke, they realized she had driven two and a half hours in the wrong direction. They laughed about this for years. When they reached Kentucky, they visited the Whitney Farm, where Chicaro had been bred, and asked Major Beard to show them everything related to this horse. Beard had served in the U.S. Army cavalry and was a well-known polo player, in addition to managing Green Tree Stud Farm. Daddy recalled: "What I heard and saw increased my interest in Chicaro so much that on our return to Texas I bought him and several of his daughters. . . . After racing Chicaro at home and studying him carefully, I saw that a good many of his colts were winning and I decided on the dual venture of giving him a chance with some real good Thoroughbred mares, but still sticking firmly to the idea of top conformation that could be used for many purposes." In 1932 we visited Mr. E. R. Bradley's Idle Hour stud and I saw Black Helen. I never forgot her!

SPORT OF KINGS

Racing with parimutuel betting was legalized in Texas in 1934. Kingsville had racing complete with grandstands, ladies and little girls in hats and gloves, and plenty of horses. Sadly, in 1937 the betting was made illegal. The Kingsville track accommodated training for King Ranch and a few match races, but after World War II it became a football field for the Texas College of Arts and Industries (now Texas A&M University at Kingsville).

EARLY WINNERS

In the mid-1930s my parents were at the races in Saratoga, New York, when Daddy purchased a number of outstanding Thoroughbreds from Morton Schwartz.

Helen C. Kleberg and Bob Kleberg Jr. holding illustration used on cover of *Time*, 1947

The large purchase attracted attention. "It was almost a heist. Right there, in front of the Saratoga regulars, the new man led off more good horses than most men own in a lifetime. . . .The top-priced Sunset Gun became the second dam of King Ranch's champions High Gun and Stymie and ancestress of other stakes winners; the Clock Tower/Gun Play filly was Dawn Play, the first champion Kleberg raced; and Science became the dam of Santa Anita Derby winner Ciencia and ancestress of other stakes winners."[49]

The ranch's early Thoroughbred winners were fillies, including Split Second, our first stakes winner; Ciencia, the first filly to win the Santa Anita Derby; and Dawn Play, which won the Acorn, the Oaks, and the American Derby. The extraordinary success of these horses, along with Daddy's work developing the Thoroughbred breed, led to his election in 1939 to the Jockey Club, which was responsible for registering and improving the breed in the United States. He later became a trustee of the New York Racing Association. He was also a founding member of the nonprofit Keeneland Racing Association.

DAWN PLAY

I became aware of the Depression in May 1937, when my parents and I traveled to New York. We always stayed at the Ambassador in New York City. My mother and I went into Bonwit Teller, where we looked at evening dresses. I asked her to buy one. I'll always remember what she said: "We can't right now, but someday we will. No one can buy anything right now." As far as I knew, we had everything we needed—ponies, food, an occasional ice-cream cone, roundups and Christmas. I do, however, recall occasionally asking Santa Claus for something extra and my mother reminding me, "We only ask him for one thing."

On that same trip, we went to Belmont. The June 3 *New York Herald Tribune* reported, "Dawn Play under L. Balaski's perfect ride won the twenty-first running of the Coaching Club American Oaks of a mile and three furlongs, at Belmont Park."[50] After the race, Daddy and

Max Hirsch, the trainer, let me hold the end of the shank to lead Dawn Play into the Winner's Circle. I saw more cash that day than I had ever seen before. My father took his personal winnings and bought my mother a pin with a blue stone with a horse carved in it, mounted with platinum and diamonds. This was a special time for my parents, especially since the Depression and the drought had been going on for so long.

Dawn Play also won the Acorn Stakes and defeated Case Ace in the American Derby. Regrettably, lightning would change her destiny in the barn at Saratoga. She was preparing to run against the famed War Admiral, but a powerful bolt blew out the lights and knocked her and several other horses out of their stalls into the alleyway. None of the animals were killed, but Dawn Play's legs swelled up after the lightning episode. She was brought to the ranch in Texas.

BOLD VENTURE

My father purchased Bold Venture from Morton Schwartz in 1939. Max Hirsch had trained him. He had won the Kentucky Derby and the Preakness Stakes before bowing a tendon, ending his career. However, Daddy recognized potential in him for breeding. As late as 1996, Bold Venture was the only horse to both win the Kentucky Derby and sire two sons that won it, Assault and Middleground. He also sired many stakes-winning daughters.

ASSAULT

A filly named Igual proved to be a vital link in one of the greatest racehorse stories in America. By Equipoise, and out of Incandescent, Igual at first caused Daddy some serious concerns. He said, "We had to hold her up while she was being suckled. I thought for a while we would have to destroy her." He recalled that, as much as he hated to do it, he would have had her destroyed if it

Bold Venture, sire of Assault and Middleground, at Santa Gertrudis

Bob Kleberg Jr. and Helen C. Kleberg at Churchill Downs, 1946

Bob Kleberg Jr. and George Blackwell, Annual Derby Lunch, Press Club in London

Max Hirsch, chief King Ranch trainer of Thoroughbreds, and Bob Kleberg Jr., 1950s

hadn't been for Caesar: "He was very patient and he kept watching her and studying her, and he asked me to give her a little more time. One day he said to Dr. Northway, 'Throw her down and go all over her, I believe you'll find she has an abscess.'" Sure enough, the doctor found an abscess under the stifle. Once he drained it, she recovered quickly."

Igual remained small and frail and was never trained. Daddy bred her as a two-year-old to Bold Venture, which produced Assault. When he was a weanling, Assault stepped on a sharp object, damaging the frog and wall of his right forefoot, and he became clubfooted. Max Hirsch, the ranch's trainer, remarked that when he received Assault at Belmont Park in the spring of 1945, "I never thought he'd train at all with that foot. I even wondered why they had sent him up from the ranch." He designed a special plate for Assault's injured foot, though, and the young horse improved. Sometime later, Hirsch recalled, "When he walks or trots, you'd think he was going to fall down."[51] Hirsch, who was from Fredericksburg, Texas, started out breaking colts and being a jockey, and later he became a respected trainer. He trained for King Ranch and other horse owners, who had their best horses with him. They also sent horses to his son, Buddy W. J. Hirsch, until he retired.

On May 4, 1946, Assault was ready to run in the Kentucky Derby. Many people spend a fortune and a lifetime trying to have a horse in that race. To win is an accomplishment few ever achieve. The Depression was over, everyone was back from the war, the spirit in America was high, and everybody was optimistic. Churchill Downs was the place to be, evidenced by the largest crowd ever. At the start, Assault was very far back. Then, with Warren Mehrtens riding, he flew past Knockdown and Spy Song, winning the race by eight lengths. It was excitement beyond belief!

A week later, in the Preakness Stakes, the outcome looked uncertain. Early on, Assault was sixth in the ten-horse field. He went after the leaders at the far turn and managed to pull ahead by four lengths with just an eighth of a mile to go. Then he tired a little, winning by a neck. The King Ranch colors were immediately painted on the jockey statuette atop the Preakness cupola. The owner, the trainer, the help, and everyone involved in the victory had champagne that day at the winning stable.

Then it was on to Belmont for the final race of the coveted Triple Crown. The Belmont track was one and a half miles around, and some believed it was too far for Assault, considering his weak finish in the Preakness. But when he galloped across the finish amid cheering crowds, he had won by three lengths. He was the seventh horse in the history of U.S. Thoroughbred racing to claim the Triple Crown.

Assault had a great race against Stymie and Galorette in the Butler Handicap. They bumped him from both sides and literally lifted him off the track, while their jockeys hit him across the face. Stymie came from behind to lead, only to be beaten by Assault at the finish line. When it was over, I asked Daddy, "Aren't you going to lodge a complaint?" "No," he said. "We won and it wouldn't be good for racing." What a brave, tough little horse Assault was!

During his career, this so-called "clubfooted comet" had forty-two starts and finished first in eighteen, second in six, and third in seven races. After proving to be sterile, despite all scientific knowledge of the time, Assault was retired on King Ranch in 1948. He was later inducted into the Thoroughbred Hall of Fame at Saratoga Springs and the Texas Racing Hall of Fame. Visitors came to the ranch from all over the world to see him. This remarkable animal, which had overcome tremendous odds, provided great encouragement, inspiration, and thrills to countless fans for years to come. Among the fan letters that arrived at the King Ranch office was this one from fifteen-year-old Denny Bowden:

> I wish like crazy that I had been old enough to realize and know the value of the world-renowned horse when I was just two.

But even though I missed out on the actual thrill of seeing him, I can still love him as much as if he were my own. I speak from my heart, Mr. and Mrs. Kleberg, when I tell of my love for the son of Bold Venture. He represents to me the true glory of Thoroughbred horse racing, the horse who overcame great obstacles to become the greatest animal on the track, the world over.

KING RANCH KENTUCKY
Beginning in the 1930s, King Ranch Thoroughbreds were shipped to and from Howard Rouse's farm near Midway, Kentucky. Howard, Daddy's close friend and college classmate, knew Thoroughbreds, the people of that region, and the racehorse business, and his expertise helped convince Daddy to extend King Ranch land to Kentucky. In 1946, the year Assault won the Kentucky Derby, shortly after the death of Col. Edward R. Bradley of Idle Hour Farm, one of the country's most successful Thoroughbred breeders, Howard told my father that Bradley's heirs wanted to settle the estate promptly. He suggested that the property would be well worth the investment. Daddy didn't think King Ranch needed all those horses or that large a place, so he convinced Jock Whitney and Ogden Phipps to form a syndicate with King Ranch to buy the Bradley estate, then disperse what they did not want.

King Ranch kept 650 acres that had been used primarily for cattle and farming. Daddy determined that the farm would be a safe place for a nucleus herd of the ranch's new breed of cattle. It would serve as a kind of insurance against the outbreak of hoof-and-mouth disease in Mexico, should it spread into South Texas. Daddy often said that the Bradley land King Ranch acquired was "not horse sick." The rest of the land was developed into fine Thoroughbred farms for others as well.

Though this Kentucky investment was a great asset, Daddy continued to raise Thoroughbreds in South Texas. Years later, he said: "With a colt raised in Texas all the way through you have a better chance of raising a classic horse than you do in Kentucky. For some reason or other, I think horses raised in those big pastures and in that hot and dry climate are stronger. I don't know if they are sounder, but they are certainly stronger."[52]

MIDDLEGROUND
On May 6, 1950, my mother, again ill, wrote in her journal: "Cool and windy – 90 degrees. 3:15 – Kentucky Derby – Middleground won – received many telephone calls – Big House for dinner." Middleground was King Ranch's second Kentucky Derby winner and had been raised in Texas. His jockey, Billy Boland of Corpus Christi, who learned to ride at King Ranch, was an apprentice and the youngest at that time to win the Derby.

In the mid-1950s, several years after Middleground had won the Kentucky Derby and the Belmont, my father was honored by the Thoroughbred Club of America. Max Hirsch, who introduced Daddy at the event, said: "He has already won more races than anybody I know of who has been in the business the same length of time. He has won practically every race in the country. Some people in a lifetime don't win any of them. Hell, he's won the Belmont twice, for instance, and some people who have been racing all their lives have never been in the money in the Belmont."

GALLANT BLOOM
My father's involvement in Thoroughbreds continued throughout his life. In 1966 he bred another champion, Gallant Bloom. Edward Bowen wrote that she was "co-champion juvenile filly at two and clearly the champion filly three years old and up at three in 1969. She is by Gallant Man, a Belmont winner that Kleberg considers one of the best horses to have raced in recent years."[53] Gallant Man was owned by Ralph Lowe of Midland, Texas. By this time my daughter Helen Alexander was starting to work with Daddy with breeding plans.

120

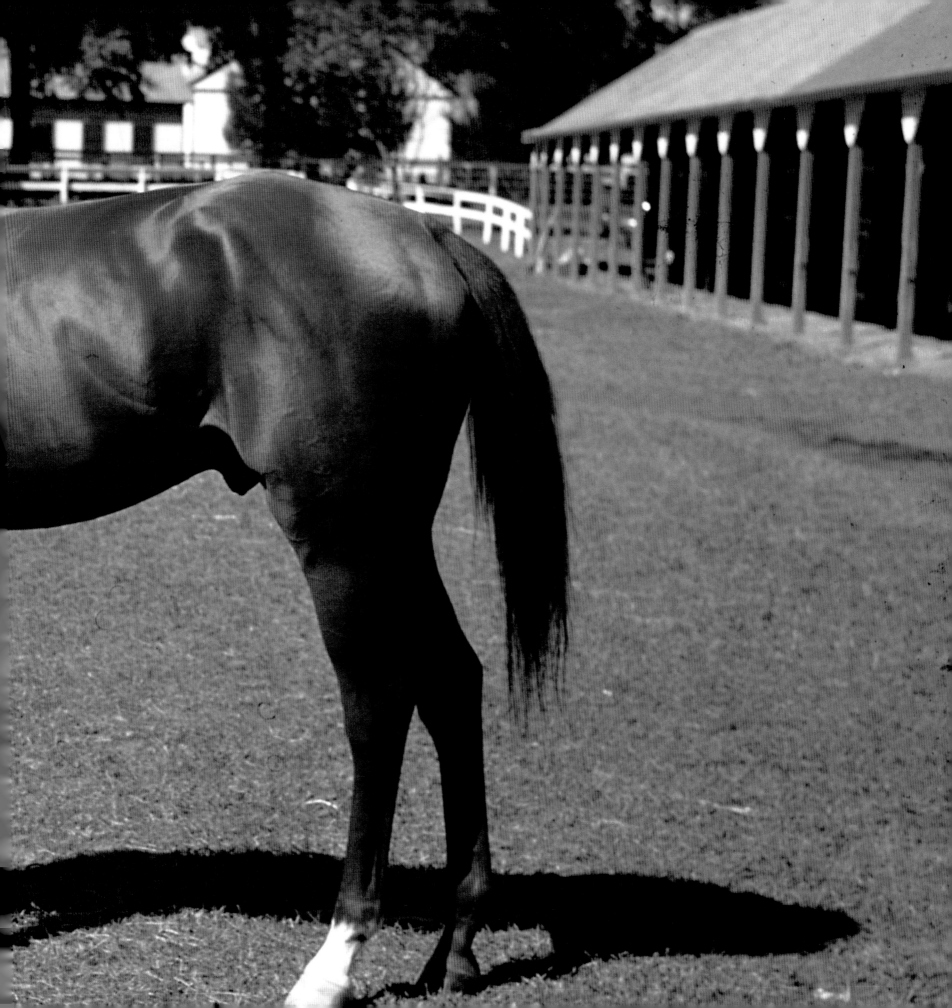

121

BELMONT PARK   JUNE 10, 1950

Mike Sirico Photo

KING RANCH owner   *"Middleground"*   MAX HIRSCH, trainer
                      WILLIAM   BOLAND up

122

Hazards

Fighting predators, parasites,
deficiency, and disease

Threats to livestock

Captain King put together one of the greatest land and livestock enterprises in this country's history. In doing so, he and his Kineños rode herd on the stock and protected the families as best they could from bandits and soldiers. They branded the thousands of cattle gathered for trail drive delivery with positive identification. At first there were no fences, but when barbed wire became available, King finished the fencing he had started with wood to enclose all of his ranch land. In his lifetime there were wooden corrals at the Santa Gertrudis headquarters. Robert Kleberg I cross-fenced for better control of breeding herds and the ability to segregate animals or rest pastures.

King Ranch cattle being dipped as they are loaded onto a railcar, 1920s

TEXAS FEVER

During the 1870s, in the last years of the trail drives to Kansas, a disease killed many local cattle near where trail herds passed. It was said that they died of Texas fever, so Texas cattle were forbidden to cross into Kansas. The market broke in the 1880s.

In the 1880s Robert Kleberg I studied and researched the disease and its path. He had noted that the fine bulls of British breed origin that he brought to Santa Gertrudis soon suffered the same symptoms as the Kansas cattle. He noticed fat ticks on the sick and dying stock and suspected that the ticks were the carriers of the sickness.

With the help of his brother Rudolph and nephew Caesar Kleberg, he was able to persuade the USDA to send a scientist to identify the cause of the fever. The scientists soon identified *Margaropus annulatus*, a tick that dies in very cold weather.

The State of Texas recognized Grandfather Kleberg's leadership and determination by appointing him in 1893 secretary of the newly created Livestock Sanitary Commission. Further using King Ranch as a laboratory, Grandfather arranged for the construction of pens with dipping vats that totally immersed cattle. With the USDA's help, various dips were tried. He theorized that if the ticks were killed, they could no longer spread the disease. An arsenic solution was the dip of choice. It did no harm to the cattle, but it cleared out the ticks. Not everyone agreed, at first, to use the procedure, but soon the state was free of Texas fever. In more recent times, outbreaks of ticks have been brought under control by using portable sprayers with insecticide other than the old tried-and-true arsenic.

The only mishap I ever heard of with these deep dipping vats was a young boy who fell into a vat and drowned before he was missed.

ARGENTINE PENS

In 1929, Daddy and my mother took their official honeymoon, by ship to Argentina. While they were touring the countryside, Daddy noticed stockmen working cattle in special sorting pens; their sharp corners had been removed to prevent bruising. He was so impressed with how these pens worked that he purchased a set and shipped them home. They became the *calera* working pens at Santa Gertrudis, a model for the future.

These pens were designed so that men standing above the stock could open and close gates, sorting the animals into different directions. Daddy added a new dimension—scales—and the ability to weigh one animal at a time. If you decided you didn't want to weigh the animal, it just passed over the scale and into the dipping vat or into a pen on either side. You could "cut" cattle up to seven different ways. These pens were of great interest to livestock producers around the United States and elsewhere.

The American National Livestock Association sent a request from H. R. Smith, of the National Livestock Loss Prevention Board, to the Texas and Southwestern Cattle Raisers Association in 1936. Mr. Smith was interested in securing blueprints for these pens: "Mr. Mollin wrote Mr. Smith some time ago telling him about these pens and the fact that the sharp corners had been removed to prevent bruising. The loss prevention board is planning to publish an illustrated pamphlet covering the results of their surveys on livestock losses and would like to use pictures of the King Ranch pens, if they could secure permission to do so."[54]

SCREWWORMS

One of the most costly pests to King Ranch and other U.S. livestock producers was the screwworm. The parasitic fly parent lays its eggs in fresh wounds of livestock or on newborns' umbilical cords. The thousands of hatched larvae feed on the animal's live flesh. I remember a sickening odor coming from animals being eaten alive by screwworms. If not treated, these flesh-eating worms would kill their host.

King Ranch cowboys were constantly on guard for any sign of these deadly parasites. When an infected animal was found, it was roped, treated, and released.

Fortunately, someone discovered that female screwworm flies only mate once. A laboratory was set up to sterilize the male flies, which were then tossed out of small airplanes in porous boxes that released them in ranching country. Daddy followed his father's example in seeing this practice instituted, and now carried forward, by Tobin Armstrong and other members of the Texas and Southwestern Cattle Raisers Association. Occasionally there are reports of this deadly pest reappearing, so constant vigilance is still necessary.

MINERAL EXPERIMENTS

In the 1930s and 1940s, South Texas grasses often lacked sufficient protein and minerals for the proper health of livestock. The lack of nutrition resulted in a debilitating condition in cattle known as "creeps," similar to osteoarthritis. To determine the cause of this devastating malady, Daddy approved a research program in the 1930s conducted by the Bureau of Animal Industry, the Texas Agricultural Experiment Station of Texas A&M University, and King Ranch. Research showed that there was a widespread deficiency of phosphorus in the grasses. A controlled feeding trial was designed to determine how seriously the deficiency affected cattle and whether supplying them with trace minerals would provide any benefit. "King Ranch made such a test possible by providing the necessary cattle and equipment on a part of the ranch that the grass analyses had indicated to be one of the most deficient in phosphorus."[55]

As the studies continued, my father wrote Tom Armstrong to inform him of the results of the practice Caesar Kleberg had first suggested in 1943: adding disodium phosphate to the diet of the cattle. "This is the first time that we have been able to raise the phosphorus in the blood stream to the desired level, by put-

Dick Kleberg Jr. and cowboys discussing mineral experiment, 1940s

Cow with "creeps," caused by lack of phosphorus in diet

ting the material in self-feeders. . . . It worked out far above expectations." In the past, ranch management had tried to supplement the diet with the addition of bone meal, which contains phosphorus. Daddy continued: "As the percentage of phosphorus in the disodium is about the same as bone meal and it has no taste whatsoever, it did not occur to me that any good could come from feeding it that way; however, Caesar has tried it and the blood tests are very gratifying. The cattle are in wonderful condition."

It turned out that the phosphorus in the disodium phosphate was more soluble than the phosphorus in the bone meal, and it was more effective. The studies showed that feeding soluble phosphate supplements to cattle in their water supply eliminated all symptoms of aphosphorosis. Daddy estimated that the calf crops were increased at least 25 percent by this practice.

Bob Kleberg Jr. at the pens, 1950s

FOOT-AND-MOUTH DISEASE

Foot-and-mouth, a costly viral disease, is highly communicable among cattle, hogs, sheep, deer, and goats. Its symptoms include blisters around the mouth, swollen feet, respiratory trouble, reduced appetite, and lameness. On Christmas day in 1946, the disease was discovered in Mexico. Texas cattlemen were fearful that it might cross the border, wiping out entire cattle herds and resulting in losses in the millions of dollars.

Rancher and longtime family friend Tobin Armstrong recalled, "My brother, John, had written several articles predicting that the Department of Agriculture's approach would be to allow Brazilian cattle, which were infected with the disease, into Mexico." This would create a dangerous problem that violated the sanitary convention the United States had with

Mexico and Brazil. "Clinton Anderson, the Department of Agriculture's head, took the position that there wasn't any danger and that this particular convention was just a tactic Texas cattlemen were using to keep foreign beef out of the United States."

At our table or when Daddy was on the phone, foot-and-mouth disease was the topic day and night. The disease was a major focus for ranchers during the 1947 Texas and Southwestern Cattle Raisers Association convention in El Paso, though members disagreed on how to handle it. Some worried about its spread in the United States, while others wanted to avoid going against the government's stance. U.S. government reports indicated that Mexico was capable of stopping the spread of foot-and-mouth on its own, but Daddy and Uncle Tom weren't willing to accept this. What Daddy proposed ignited a volatile discussion. "In order to strengthen our own position," he said, "a clause should be added to the resolution"—which the association had proposed to address the disease— "simply pointing out that we still feel and believe that the only sure and safe method of eliminating foot and mouth disease is by the slaughter method, and I so move, Mr. Chairman, that the clause be added as a rider or amendment."[56]

Since the U.S. Department of Agriculture and Mexican government officials had already agreed to address foot-and-mouth, some in TSCRA leadership believed approval of the resolution might ignite an international conflict. They called for caution. An old friend of my father's, Claude McCan of Victoria, Texas, said, "I think we'd better leave it as it is and have confidence in their leadership. Let's not bung up the idea by passing something like this." He looked at Daddy and said, "I think you should withdraw your motion, which I ask you to do. The [Mexican government] are going to do the best they can."

"I certainly don't think so!" Daddy said.

As the discussion continued, Jay Taylor of Amarillo spoke up: "The greatest living authority on foot-and-mouth disease is Dr. Moeller, and . . . he says the only known method [of containment] is immediate slaughter of foot-and-mouth disease cattle, so why the hell shouldn't we say that in this resolution?"

Claude McCan said, "You're dealing with the Mexican government now, so let's don't hamper them. What we think is right, and I agree one hundred percent, but let's let them have a free hand."

Daddy retorted, "My thought is to give them a free hand by restricting them and saying we would not be satisfied with anything short of what should be done. This is not the time for us to be playing around."[57]

INVESTIGATING MEXICO

Tobin Armstrong recalled that "tensions were really high, but Uncle Tom Armstrong and Bob Kleberg weren't willing to accept the USDA reports," which claimed that Mexico was successfully containing the disease. He continued, "On their own they employed a retired field inspector from the Cattle Raisers Association and directed him, 'You go into Mexico and find out what's going on and report back to us.' "

When the investigator returned from Vera Cruz, he reported his findings, the essence of which was that Mexican officials were not destroying contaminated cattle. Tobin said, "They took money the American government had provided them to buy cattle that were

then to be destroyed and buried in quick lime." Instead of destroying them, he explained, officials kept the money and expropriated the cattle, hauling them into Mexico City, where they were sold.

TSCRA members who had supported the USDA program now agreed that a serious national problem existed. Daddy created a detailed plan, which came to be known as the Texas Plan, to stop the epidemic in Mexico, and the TSCRA forwarded it to the U.S. Department of Agriculture. The plan proposed replacing infected cattle in southern Mexico with cattle from northern Mexico, thereby offering that region a new market and improving the historically inferior cattle in the south. It argued that the policy of vaccination adopted by a joint U.S.-Mexico commission had no advantages, particularly since dangerous carriers—exposed or sick livestock—would likely be vaccinated along with the rest. The vaccine had no curative effect and no value in terms of complete eradication, and carriers would simply continue to spread the disease.

By now the disease had spread through more than half of Mexico, despite the fact that the U.S. government had spent $34 million trying to eradicate it. My father was quoted in the March 11, 1948, *New York World-Telegram*: "The administration had everything it wanted, but what with the buck-passing between the State Department and the Department of Agriculture, we have gotten nowhere in 18 months. Either it's been done wrong, or it can't be done, and I'm not willing to say it can't be done."[58]

As a result of several years of cooperative efforts between the livestock producers in Texas and Mexico, state and federal government agencies, and political forces, the plan was implemented, preventing foot-and-mouth disease from entering Texas. Disaster had been averted, with Mexico free of foot-and-mouth disease as well. Lifelong friendships were saved too!

125

Ranching Pleasures

Entertainment, hunting, and camping

Hunting and other diversions

LOS AMIGOS CAMP

As young men, my father and Tom Armstrong established a special campsite at Norias, the ranch's southernmost division. They named it Los Amigos Camp, or "Friends Camp." Each December, they left their work to go to Los Amigos, where they would rough it, hunting and socializing. Uncle Tom referred to these excursions as "clearing my head." They would come back home long enough to spend Christmas day with their families and then return. The ritual daily shower was taken in a stall that was open to the sky. Though it had hot and cold water, you could tell the difference only when there was ice on the water tank; at those times the water out of the well was warmer. Meager in physical conveniences (by their desire), the camp was restricted to use by them and a few hardy friends until Daddy married my mother.

She joined the men and soon designed a grand wall made of live oak logs and brush to break the winter winds. Several large tarps provided covered shelter where they could cook, eat, and sit. The campfire, which was just outside the tarps, was ringed with bull skulls for seating. Two tents, one for the men and the other for the women, were put up for privacy and comfort. There were also tents for food and spirits and for the men who took care of everyone. There were riding horses and milk cows, as well as hunting cars and a screened game tent.

ALL IS NOT LOST

I was sound asleep in my cot at Los Amigos Camp when my mother and father got into an argument near the campfire. Both were strong-willed, and before long they were in the middle of a discussion so acrimonious that it seemed as if separation was the only solution. Uncle Tom sat on a bull's head nearby, trying to stay out of it, until it appeared that my parents' world might shortly be coming to an end. He did something drastic. Without warn-

ing, he pulled his pistol from its holster and fired, shooting an old camp dog in a hind leg. Startled, the dog let out a yelp and ran off into the darkness, whereupon my parents immediately turned on Tom. Their marriage was saved, and the dog recovered. No one remembered what the argument was about, but in years to come, when my parents and Uncle Tom observed a tense situation, they would look at each other and say, "Do you think it's time to shoot a dog?"

HUNTING CARS

To take their friends hunting on the ranch, Daddy and Uncle Tom designed special hunting cars. The earlier ones carried bird dogs in boxes on the running boards and had loose leather scabbards for rifles and shotguns tied on the sides. Over time, the cars became more elaborate, with compartments for food and drink, coats, and ammunition, but no dogs. Uncle Dick had Buick build a hunting car to his specifications. It was a masterpiece and is currently in the King Ranch Museum in Kingsville.

ANNUAL SOCIAL AFFAIRS

Each fall and winter, my parents hosted hunting and camping on the ranch that could last from days to weeks. Their guests included family and friends, as well as business, government, and military leaders from around the world. From Los Amigos, visitors would divide into small groups and depart in different directions in search of quail, dove, deer, and turkey, meeting later for lunch in the field. Most enjoyed the camaraderie as much as the hunt. My father was often working cattle, so he hunted only in the late afternoon.

Helen C. Kleberg

Caesar Kleberg (center) and friends, 1920s

In September 1940, Daddy wrote that, in preparation for a visit from Walter C. Teagle, president of Standard Oil Company, he "spent yesterday with Caesar at Norias and saw a good many quail when I was driving down, so I think that we will have a good quail season this fall. It is a little bit early yet to be sure, but the signs are pretty good. Caesar has hatched out about 30 wild guineas, that he knows of, and it looks as if he might finally succeed in trying to establish the guinea down there." Entries from my mother's journal also reflect the importance of hunting:

> January 2, 1948. Olga & Harry Weiss arrive in the morning on the train – Shooting – Lunch at cow camp – Henrietta and Tom join us for lunch and dinner
>
> January 3. Lunch in camp – shooting quail
>
> January 4. Lunch in camp – shooting quail with Olga & Harry Weiss
>
> January 5. Lunch in cow camp – shooting quail with Olga – I killed a big rattlesnake

My parents hosted numerous parties in camp and at home that included several young Rockefellers and racing friends. In the late 1950s, my father received the following note from President Eisenhower: "Yesterday, Nate Twining called to tell me that he had brought back from Texas a quantity of quail, venison and turkey—all provided through your kindness. I gather that the White House is bursting at the seams, and of course I anticipate a lot of good eating when I return there the end of this week. With best wishes to you and Helen for the finest possible New Year and, as always, warm regards."

My mother loved competition, whether it was jumping fences on the back of a Thoroughbred, following hounds through the woods, or shooting. She described a good day with her shotgun on February 18, 1962: "Pigeon shoot at Matamoros – Lady's Day – First place, Helen C. Kleberg, ten out of ten birds. Second Place, Anne Armstrong, nine out of ten. Third Place, Mary Lewis Kleberg, eight out of ten."

131

132

134

135

60

141

A Wider Frontier

Cuba, Australia, Argentina,
Brazil, Venezuela, Morocco, and Spain

King Ranch international

From left: President
Anastasio Somoza of
Nicaragua, Helen C.
Kleberg, and Bob Kleberg
Jr. in Nicaragua

Helen K. (Kleberg)
Alexander with son John
Alexander on Topsy

Today, King Ranch operations are focused mainly in Texas and Florida. While Daddy was at the helm he distributed King Ranch cattle and horses far beyond their South Texas pastures. In 1946, he established ranches in Pennsylvania and Kentucky, and some years later he took King Ranch into Florida. He was also responsible for establishing and directing King Ranch operations in Cuba, Australia, Brazil, Argentina, Venezuela, Spain, and Morocco.

Daddy believed that wars were caused by the hunger for energy. In the case of humans, that meant protein; machines, on the other hand, needed fossil fuel. Land that could not be used for farming—that is, land that was rocky, dry, steep, or remote—could support cattle with grass and brush that people could not otherwise utilize.

Many opportunities for foreign investment came to my father's attention. Before he committed King Ranch to adding new properties, he followed a strict procedure. The prospective countryside was evaluated from the air and then the ground. Keenly observant, Daddy noted the size of trees within their species, which helped him determine the soil's fertility. If he noticed that the region's stray dogs were fat, that was a good indication of few parasites. He was also concerned, of course, about the availability of water.

Daddy cultivated relationships with leaders of other countries and listened to their assessments of their governments and resources. Leroy Denman Jr., former president of King Ranch, recalls: "Most of the time Bob Kleberg would personally meet the political officials of the country where he was planning to conduct business. . . . Bob thoroughly enjoyed going to a new country and evaluating its potential for beef production."

CUBA

A 1952 entry in my mother's diary announced, "The Cuban venture is on!" Leroy Denman Jr. recalls, "We had discussed the possibility of establishing a ranch in Cuba during Helenita's wedding reception, in 1949. Bob believed then that it was as safe to invest in Cuba as it was in America." John Cypher explains the project: "King Ranch went to Cuba at the behest of two brothers, George and Riondo Braga of New York, whose family, back to the Spanish colonial era, had been sugar producers in the provinces of Oriente and Camaguey. Forming a joint venture with the Manati Sugar Company, one of the Braga subsidiaries, Bob set out to create a beef factory in the brush land and forest near the north central Camaguey coast."[59]

During one of his first trips, Daddy met Gustavo de los Reyes, who would become a lifelong friend. Gustavo recalls their meeting:

Alfonso Fanjul asked if I would give him a hand since he and several others were going to have some Texans from the King Ranch visiting their place and looking over the country. Alfonso also informed me they were planning a joint venture and since their property bordered my ranch, La Caridad, I told them of course I would cooperate.

On the day the King Ranch people were to arrive at my ranch, I jumped in the plane. However, due to some bad weather I arrived late; the whole party had already left my ranch headquarters. To catch up with them, I asked for my favorite horse, and the cowboy said, "Impossible." "How come?" I responded. "Well," he said, "one of the Texans liked your horse and he took it. There was no way of avoiding that, except by shooting him."

Very displeased, I mounted another and set out to meet the Texans. I galloped in the direction the visiting party had taken. After a while, way in the distance, I saw my horse Caramelo. As I approached the group I was struck by the rider on my horse and the old hat he was wearing. I said, "That's my horse, you know!" The stranger gave a disarming smile and said, "And a damned good one too! I'm Bob Kleberg." We shook hands and became friends forever.

On April 11, 1952, my mother wrote in her diary, "Operation Noah's Ark is on—horses and equipment loaded onto the cargo ship, *Nancy Lykes*, bound for Cuba." Shortly thereafter, my parents traveled to Cuba, accompanied by Leroy Denman Jr., his wife, Flea, and Mary Lewis and Dick Kleberg Jr. My mother recorded some of their experiences: "We first stopped at Santa Beatrice Ranch, met Bernabe Sanchez and had lunch." Bernabe had a beautiful herd of Santa Gertrudis on his plantation, which had been in his family since Cuba's earliest colonial times. The group flew to Camaguey and motored through the countryside until, as my mother put it, "the road came to a dead end." They climbed aboard a train car that seemed to have "been fitted out of a hog car" and traveled a narrow-gauge railroad to King Ranch's newest property.

During one of my parents' many trips to Cuba, some friends invited my mother to shop in Havana. At this time in their lives, with ranch properties in Cuba, Brazil, and Australia, my parents were traveling quite a bit. My mother said, "You know, when you visit these countries the people there are very interested in what you are wearing. I need to have some nice, appropriate clothes for these occasions."

She met Erique, Havana's star designer. When he inquired what she was looking for, she said, "I'd like to have something in green."

"Madame," he said, "green is never chic. Black or brown, but never green!"

She purchased a skirt, a top, and some dinner clothes. They were so tight she couldn't sit down. Erique informed her, "You must suffer to be beautiful! This is the size you need to be. You will learn!" She did.

Becerra, King Ranch's joint venture in Cuba, was grazing about 7,600 head of cattle on the north side of the island when my mother wrote in her journal on June 30, 1959, "Disaster has struck in Cuba!" She was referring to the actions of Fidel Castro, backed by the Soviet Union. A devastating revolution was under way. Cuba's political, governmental, business, and social structures were failing under Castro's control. Within three months, his soldiers arrived at the entrance to Becerra. My mother's October 1 entry states, "Cuba confiscated the ranch!" King Ranch lost most of what they invested, including the cattle, which were soon sent to Russia, but friendship endured!

AUSTRALIA

Daddy became interested in Australia when Lew Douglas, the former ambassador to the Court of St. James and an Arizona rancher, introduced him to William Sidney Robinson. Robinson was Australia's leading businessman and consultant to governments, as well as a personal friend of Winston Churchill and Bernard Baruch. Robinson inspired Daddy to examine the possibilities in Australia. He introduced him to Sir Rupert Clarke, a baronet, pastoralist, and investment banker. He also introduced Daddy to Sam Hordern,

Bob Kleberg Jr. (front left) at Becerra, Cuba, 1952

In Australia, 1952

From left: foreman, Peter Baillieu, W. S. and Gertrude Robinson, and Bob Kleberg Jr. in Australia, 1952

Lady Katharine Clarke (Mrs. Rupert Clarke), 1956

Sidney Royal Show, judging Santa Gertrudis cow, 1956

one of Australia's leading agri-businessmen, and to Peter Baillieu, a breeder and station manager. Clarke asked Daddy to think about a partnership to ship a top stud herd of Santa Gertrudis cattle to Australia. Clarke, Hordern, and Baillieu became the original King Ranch Australia partners.

In late 1951, my father, in collaboration with Dr. Albert O. Rhoad and Dr. J. K. Northway, the King Ranch veterinarian, cut out 206 heifers and 75 bulls from Santa Gertrudis, forming the foundation herd. On May 16, seventeen stock cars filled with cattle pulled out of the loading chute at King Ranch's Caesar Pens, arriving in San Pedro, California, five days later. Jim McBride, the foreman of the Encino division was in charge. In addition to his wife, who went along "just for the trip," McBride was supported by a work party of seven. The first joint Australian-American venture to establish a foundation herd of a new breed of cattle was under way.

Although good planning had alleviated many challenges, no one could have foreseen what lay ahead for these animals and their handlers. Before they could sail, the Sailors Union of the Pacific called a strike and walked out, causing a delay in the departure of the two ships assigned to transport the cattle. Meanwhile, the cattle were quarantined on the train due to an Australian regulation that would not allow them to touch ground in California. On May 26, as the first vessel, *M.S. Kanangoor*, was being loaded, several bulls broke away, jumping into the water. One swam for the main harbor channel. One of the men chased the bull in a water taxi and managed to rope and tether him to some piling. But the bull broke free and headed into the waterfront's industrial district. Pedestrians ran for safety. "Finally, police and cowboys subdued him.

Three of the other bulls . . . swam to the Marine Corps Reserve headquarters island in the harbor. There, some of the Texas cowboys guarding the consignment, helped by marines, engaged in an impromptu rodeo."[60]

Without waiting for the escaped cargo to board, the ship sailed on schedule that afternoon, carrying forty-five bulls, 27,000 pounds of feed for consumption en route, and bedding straw. At the end of July, nearly two months later, 201 heifers and 27 bulls were herded onto the Sierras. Three and half months after leaving King Ranch, the precious cargo arrived in Melbourne. The animals were quarantined on Goode Island; after about a month, government officials decided the long trip was adequate quarantine time. Since the cattle showed no signs of warbles, they were released.

ARGENTINA

During a trip to Argentina in August 1961, my mother wrote, "Bob back from the province of Corrientes – bought Aguay." This new property totaled about 40,000 acres and was located about 500 miles north of Buenos Aires. The investment was King Ranch's third in Argentina. The others, El Abolengo and Carmen, were on the border of the provinces of Santa Fe and Buenos Aires, about 200 miles west of the city of Buenos Aires. Presently Aguai is owned by my daughter Emory, who bought it from King Ranch Argentina.

Yugilbar Castle, Australia, 1956

Bobby Shelton and Bob Kleberg Jr., Brazil, 1958

Leroy Denman Jr. recalled: "In Argentina, Bob always paid a call on that country's president. I thought it was kind of presumptuous on his part, but he would announce himself, 'I am Bob Kleberg and I want to talk to you.' Once he gave him a long lecture on economics and told him how badly things were being run and what he ought to do about it. I was amazed at the president's positive reaction to Bob's instructions." Leroy also told a story about when Daddy was looking at land in Argentina. They were in a light airplane, flying out from Buenos Aires, and Daddy asked the pilot to fly west. About two hours later, as they neared the western edge of the country, Daddy asked the pilot to turn around. When Leroy asked why, Daddy said, "You see those haystacks down there? I don't want to ranch in any country where you have to put up hay. We have enough dry country in South Texas without going to Argentina to find more."

Leroy added, "For Bob, Argentina was the supreme challenge to his ability as a rancher and for his Santa Gertrudis cattle. He stayed clear as long as Evita and Juan Perón were in power. He believed that they had nearly destroyed the ranching industry and preferred to wait until they were out and the political forces in Argentina calmed down."

BRAZIL

By 1961, King Ranch was operating several ranches in Brazil in partnership with Swift International. The land was owned separately and amicable means for dissolving the partnership were part of the agreement. During one of my parents' visits to the Mosquito Ranch, my mother wrote in her journal, "Looking over property. Went with boatmen to look for pebbles to place on the walk and saw cattle. Went fishing with Celia, Octavio and Elizabeth. First caught small fish and then big ones. This is delicious Brazilian food!"

When my parents first went to Mosquito, the only place for them to stay was a screenless house with chickens running in and out, and an outside bathroom with a toilet that was flushed with a bucket of water. The shower was a milk can with holes punched in the top, hung high with a pull-chain. Later, a lovely house with a garden designed by landscape architect Berle Marks, whom my mother had read about and whose work she admired, served as the modern headquarters.

VENEZUELA

After Cuba fell under Castro, Gustavo de los Reyes, released from political prison in Cuba, came to the United States in the early 1960s and managed a ranch in Florida. Soon he and my father would take King Ranch into Venezuela. What a contrast from drought-ridden South Texas. Venezuela had two main seasons: December to April, which was dry, and May to November, when heavy rains inundated the region.

Gustavo located a property called Mostrenco in the northwestern part of the country, near San Felipe in the state of Yaracay. He recalled, "Since creation, this country had been a dense jungle filled with snakes, jaguars, ticks, and mosquitoes. We cleared it using bulldozers and converted it into a verdant paradise of tall emerald-green guinea grasses that looked like fans moved by the breeze. . . . Situated on a rolling mesa above sea level, its valleys were soon full of fat, impressive white Brahman and cherry-red Santa Gertrudis cattle."

King Ranch's next property in Venezuela was in El Cedral, a jungle in the state of Apure. The jungle contained hundreds of bird species, including orinoco geese, green swallows, crested bobwhite, and yellow-headed parrots. Orinoco crocodiles and anacondas stalked their prey while capybara grew to the size of pigs. Gustavo remembers the determination and technical skill Daddy used to convert this country into a valuable asset. "Nobody wanted this property," he said, "but when Bob saw it, he asked me, 'Where does all this water come from?' I told him the Andes Mountains, and he just said, 'I like it!' "

Daddy purchased it, and the owners gave him five years to pay it off. Floodwaters covered the land during certain seasons, but Daddy converted the area into fields. His efforts to ensure proper balance with nature were recognized in the April 1998 *National Geographic*: "El Cedral was once a holding of the enormous King Ranch of Texas, which had a policy of peacefully coexisting with the wildlife. Consequently, many animals have little fear of humans, drawing bird-watchers by the hundreds here every year."[61]

BIG B RANCH, FLORIDA

During the 1960s, Alvaro Sanchez, an old friend and prominent Cuban cattleman, and Walter Beinecke Jr., head of the popular S&H Green Stamp Company, invited my father to look at some muck wasteland south of Lake Okeechobee, Florida. I remember flying over this flat country with Daddy. We saw one or two deer, some birds, brownish grass, and a few scrub willows, but otherwise there didn't seem to be much. Daddy was soon convinced that this country could be an excellent place to breed single-sire herds, as moisture was constant and pastures small and easily monitored. These conditions would permit rapid genetic improvement of the Santa Gertrudis.

The grass, however, lacked the essential minerals necessary to support efficient livestock production. Also, the mosquitoes and parasites indigenous to this subtropical region carried livestock diseases, some of which are still unknown. These challenges eventually brought a halt to livestock production. Today, sugar-cane, sod, and vegetables have replaced our cattle, while hawks and owls, rather than pesticides, control rodents. Citrus is a major crop. Grandfather Kleberg would have approved.

SPAIN

The Spanish climate and ambience seemed a natural fit for Santa Gertrudis cattle and King Ranch Quarter Horses. The bird hunting was good, but the labor situation was not. I don't know why the venture wasn't ultimately a success.

MOROCCO

King Ranch extended into Morocco at the request of King Mohammed V. The king sent a representative to King Ranch to see if Daddy would consider establishing a herd of Santa Gertrudis in Morocco. After researching the region, Daddy observed a beautiful valley in the Atlas Mountains. Leroy Denman Jr. recalled that Daddy told the king, "If you can find land in this valley, I will bring cattle." But, he cautioned, "Your problem here is that the land is constantly grazed down by Berbers, who push their sheep and goats across it every time it rains, eating up all the grass."

The Moroccan government agreed to relocate the Berbers, and King Ranch brought a sizable herd to what became Ranch Adarouch. "Bob was often amused and sort of shocked as he watched the Moroccan cowboys herding cattle on foot, running over the rocky terrain in slippers and robes," Leroy said.

Although King Ranch management later sold all of the properties, Santa Gertrudis cattle and King Ranch Quarter Horses are recognized and utilized worldwide. Best of all, the wonderful friends my parents made and their families are friends of our King Ranch family.

(preceding pages)
141 Helen C. Kleberg and Bob Kleberg Jr. traveling, late 1950s

(following pages)
143 Mr. Finch and Bob Kleberg Jr. in Argentina, 1957

144 Bob Kleberg Jr. (third from left) on Nelson Rockefeller's ranch in Brazil, 1957

145 Helen C. Kleberg and Bob Kleberg Jr. hunting in Scotland, circa 1961

146 Helen C. Kleberg (right) with rifle and camera in Australia, 1956

147 Ross Douglas with Santa Gertrudis herd in Australia, 1956

148 Moving large herd of King Ranch cattle in Australia, 1950s

149 "Road train" hauling cattle in Australia, 1950s

150 Branding in Australia, 1956

151 Argentine gauchos, 1957

152 Brazilian cowboys, 1953

153 Zebu parade in Brazil, 1953

144

145

146

151

152

Family

Love of life, hard work and excellence

The strongest ties

When Daddy was a boy, travel from King Ranch was limited to horses and an occasional ride on a train or boat; there were no automobiles. Any social or work activities included the entire family. It was during this period that he was taught about land and livestock. More important, however, were the lessons he learned about respect and loyalty to his family and others. He was the next-to-youngest of five children, including Richard, Henrietta, Alice, and Sarah.

UNCLE DICK

Daddy's older brother, Richard Mifflin, whom I called Uncle Dick, was a charming people-person. A graduate of the University of Texas Law School, he served as a U.S. congressman for the 14th District of Texas from 1932 to 1944. An excellent horseman and a fine roper, Uncle Dick liked to show off his charro-trained horse. He loved breeding and fighting game chickens, and he raised acres of these birds at Santa Gertrudis and other camps on the ranch. Uncle Dick served as president of the Texas and Southwestern Cattle Raisers Association. He was also a great shot—he could shoot a hole through a coin thrown into the air. After his death, the *Robstown Record* wrote:

> His command of the Spanish language and his complete understanding of the thinking and customs of the Latin-American people placed him in a position to serve well on congressional committees assigned to the solution of inter-American problems, especially those dealing with aviation, . . . agricultural and livestock questions, . . . He loved music and would sit occasionally at the piano to play the nostalgic melodies he had learned as a boy with tears streaming down his weather-creased cheeks.[62]

Dick Jr., Uncle Dick's son, worked cattle with the rest of us cousins in the summers, but he came to be Daddy's right-hand man on the ranch after college. He was there during the hardest times.

AUNT HENRIETTA

My father's oldest sister, Henrietta, was as at home on the range as she was in New York, where she and her first husband, John Larkin, raised four children, Etta, Ida, Johnny, and Peter. When I was little, I called her Aunt Fuzzy because her hair was so curly.

After her first husband died in 1949, Henrietta married my godfather, Uncle Tom Armstrong, and returned to live in South Texas near her daughters. They had been lifelong friends. She served as chairman of the King Ranch board of directors for many years, always opening meetings with a prayer. She asked that Grandfather Kleberg's icehouse in Kingsville be preserved as a museum and archival center. Today thousands visit the King Ranch Museum each year. Her two sons-in-law, Jim Clement and John Armstrong, served as presidents of King Ranch after my father's death. Jim, who was married to Ida, served for twelve difficult years, holding all of King Ranch's properties together.

AUNT ALICE

Alice married Tom East and lived with him in the big house at Santa Gertrudis. They later set up their own ranching enterprise, San Antonio Viejo, in Hebbronville. Eventually King Ranch bought this property and Tom continued to manage it.

During World War I, there was danger in Texas as well as Europe. One morning Aunt Alice and Uncle Tom went to their ranch before daylight. Tom had gotten out of the car to catch some horses in a nearby pen when armed bandits surrounded the car. They wanted to take Alice somewhere. When Tom realized what was happening, he hid in the darkness. Aunt Alice said,

Congressman Richard M.
Kleberg (Uncle Dick)

Alice Kleberg East
(Aunt Alice)

"Let's go up to the house. There's coffee, and I'll fix you breakfast." The bandits left with her. Uncle Tom saddled a horse and rode for help.

Years later, I asked Aunt Alice, "Did you really take the bandits to your house." I will always remember her reply: "Heavens, no! Some friends had given us a bottle of champagne for our anniversary and I wasn't going to let them get it!" Can you imagine being in the middle of nowhere, surrounded by bandits, and thinking about protecting your bottle of champagne?

Alice would hang the basket that baby Tom Jr. lay in from the nearest mesquite while she worked cattle. She was tough.

When we were young, Aunt Alice took B. K. Johnson and me on several breakfast rides. She brought a frying pan, bacon, and eggs. When we stopped she would send us to gather sticks for a fire. Then she would cook our breakfast. We had wonderful times. Alice lived to be 104 years old. She and her daughter Lica are buried at San Antonio Viejo ranch, surrounded by deer and turkey. Robert continues to ranch there.

AUNT SARAH

My father adored his youngest sister, Sarah Spohn. He told me that when she was little she would often cry until the cowboys let her go on roundup with them. Being younger than the rest, she would get so tired trying to keep up that she would doze off and occasionally fall off. Her gentle horse would stop, waiting until someone came back to find her asleep on the ground.

Aunt Sarah grew up in the saddle, learning to rope, shoot, smoke cigarettes, and drink whiskey. In the late 1920s she fell in love with a tall, handsome cowboy—Henry Belton Johnson Jr. He had distinguished himself at Virginia Military Institute, where he was Top Captain of the class of 1926, the school's highest rank. After he graduated with a degree in civil engineering, and a whirlwind romance, he and Sarah were wed at Santa Gertrudis in 1928.

They hadn't been married long when Belton fell from a moving hunting car. At first he seemed uninjured, but then he started having frequent headaches.

He was diagnosed with a brain tumor. After several operations he died, leaving behind Aunt Sarah and their baby son, B. K.

Later, Aunt Sarah married Dr. Joseph H. Shelton of Kingsville. They had a son, Robert Richard (Bobby) Shelton, and a daughter, Sarita. She had big, light-blue eyes and blond curly hair and was as sweet as she looked. Doctor Shelton was sought after for everything, including delivering babies, setting broken arms, or, in my case, giving a tetanus shot for a rat bite.

He and Sarah loved going into the interior of Mexico in search of pre-Columbian artifacts. On their return from one of these trips, they found Bobby very ill with mastoid and pneumonia. Precious Sarita had died of the same illness and been buried.

Doctor Shelton had been working hard and was not feeling well. He was told to slow down, so he started going home for lunch and taking a ten-minute nap. A few days before Christmas 1938, his stepson B. K. took him coffee and found him dead. What a shock.

During an eight-year period, Aunt Sarah lost two husbands and a daughter. Her son B. K. Johnson remembers, "These continued losses just crushed her, and she withdrew from the ranch and friends. Her heart was broken." In 1942, Sarah died in an auto accident, leaving her boys orphaned. After much family discussion it was decided that they should live with their grandmother Kleberg, Mana, in the big house at Santa Gertrudis. She adored both boys and often had their company for extended periods.

B. K. AND BOBBY

B. K. Johnson and Bobby Shelton lived with Mana until her death in 1944. Once again they were alone. B. K. recalled, "Bobby and I were sitting by the pool next to the diving board and I remember Bobby saying, 'What are we going to do?' And I said, 'I don't know, Bobby.' I was eleven and he was five. I recall Uncle Bob saying, 'We'd like you two to live with us, but that decision is up to you.' Bobby and I decided it would be best if we went to live with Uncle Bob, Aunt Helen, and Helenita.

Sarah Kleberg

B. K. Johnson (standing) and Bobby Shelton, 1950s

Bob Kleberg Jr. with first-born grandchild, Helen C. Alexander

Helen C. Kleberg with grandchildren in the Santa Gertrudis swimming pool, 1950s

It was the most momentous decision of our lives."

Bobby was a charming boy. I will always remember the time I asked him to straighten up his room. Before I realized what was happening, he was sitting on the bed, telling me how to clean it up. He was good at getting people to do things. He was bright and didn't seem to have any difficulty making A's in school. To get him to work harder, my mother encouraged him to read more.

In an effort to get some idea of what he wanted to do in the future, she asked, "Bobby, don't you want to grow up to be like your father, Dr. Shelton?" He said no. "Well then, do you want to grow up to be like Uncle Bob?" Again, he said no. Then my mother said, "What do you want to grow up to be or who do you want to be like?" Bobby replied, "I want to be a little boy and play!"

B. K. and I were like brother and sister. He used to say that my beautiful friends and I gave him gray hair when he was fourteen. He was always receptive to suggestions from my mother, and they got along well. He recalls how, in August 1944, she surprised him with a trip to one of America's oldest private schools:

We had just arrived when Aunt Helen said, "I've got to go back to New York to meet your Uncle Bob." I was confused when I heard her say that because I thought we had come up so I could take a look at Deerfield Academy. But then, to my surprise, she started walking out of the room, which I didn't understand, so I followed her. "Where are you going?" she said. With you!" I said. "No, you're not. You're staying here." I've always felt that attending Deerfield Academy was a fork in the road for me. It was Aunt Helen who introduced me to this wonderful school.

GRANDCHILDREN

My parents treasured the times they spent with their grandchildren. The feeling was mutual. My daughter, Emory G. Alexander Hamilton, remembers how my mother loved to fish:

She had spinning rods and fly rods. On numerous occasions she took us to the lake where she is now buried. There we would catch nothing, and she would go to the opposite side of the lake and catch one fish after another. . . . Having grown up on the East Coast, Grandmother loved coming to Buck and Doe in Pennsylvania. She and my grandfather stayed in a house about half a mile from ours. Often we would stop by to see them before school. My grandfather would be making coffee and burning toast, and Grandmother would come down to the kitchen, smelling of orange skin cream.

After my mother died, Daddy said, "I have lost my best friend." But he knew she would have wanted him to go on and was inspired by her memory. Sustained by family and friends, he was in constant motion and communication. He took all of my children who were old enough on trips to King Ranch properties around the world, stopping off in the major cities of each country and introducing them to friends he had made over the years.

When we were living at Buck and Doe, Daddy would come up from Texas to stay with us. His visits were too short. My children always looked forward to seeing him. I will forever recall their response when I would announce that breakfast was ready. "Oh, no, Mommy," they said. "We want to go over and have hard-boiled eggs and burnt toast with Abuelito!"

Daddy would take the ranch's plane, a DC-3, to the races and to conduct business in New York, and afterward he would pick us up. On our way back to Texas, we would often stop at the farm in Kentucky. My children greatly enjoyed this, especially if the weather was warm. They loved to swim in the stock troughs where the cattle drank. Later, a swimming pool was put in and they looked forward to that as well. I knew Daddy missed my mother, so I would take my children to South Texas to spend as much time with him as possible.

One year, after we spent the Christmas holidays at the ranch, my daughter Cina stayed on. In mid-February Daddy brought her to New York, where I met them. We had lunch and visited the Museum of Natural History. Afterward, Daddy returned to King Ranch and Cina and I went home to Buck and Doe Valley Farms. Ever since that stay with my parents, Cina's love of nature has been fixed for life.

Whether it was a playful moment in the morning or a more complex learning situation, Daddy had a wonderful impact on my children's lives. He always said, "No excuses"—that was how he lived his life and expected us to live ours. Helen, my eldest, was studying pedigrees by the time she was seven. She spent many hours with Daddy learning about horses and cattle, developing an excellent eye, and learning his theories about breeding. After Daddy died, she ran the King Ranch farm in Kentucky until it was sold years later. She has her own farm now.

My son John Alexander remembers: "Grandfather always found time for his grandchildren, especially as we grew older. He loved to tickle and wrestle with us and we always had a great time when we were with him. He was always probing to learn from those around him. One of my favorite times was in the mornings when Grandfather was still wearing his pajamas. He would crawl around on his hands and knees, growling like a wolf and teasing us."

THE LAST TRIP
Throughout Daddy's life, his hunger for knowledge never ceased. In July 1974, at the age of seventy-eight, he took my three oldest children, Helen, Emory, and John, and me on a safari to Kenya, East Africa, and Botswana. Though he had visited the Serengeti some years earlier, he had never seen the Kalahari, where he wanted to observe how humans, domestic livestock, and wildlife coexisted. He was fascinated with the desert's natural balance, but he perceived its changing future. "You know, they've been doing this for thousands and thousands of years and it will soon be all disturbed by roads and transportation."

In the Kalahari, Daddy shared a more private reason for taking the trip. He needed time to make the most important decision of his life, which he did alone. He believed that after nearly sixty years of managing King Ranch, it was time for him to step down. He told me, "I think the family is at last mature enough to choose their next leader, but I'd like to be around to offer whatever help I can with the transition."

It was the last trip we took with Daddy. In August of that year he worked cattle on horseback, cutting and roping at Norias. In October he was dead from a cancerous abdominal tumor involving his pancreas.

CONTINUING LEGACY
Emory recalls that Daddy used to say that one of the greatest gifts he could give his grandchildren was the friends he had made during his lifetime. She also remembers the times she spent with him—at roundups, hunting, riding across the pastures—and the things he taught her: "After returning to Santa Gertrudis from a long trip, he had many pouches of mail waiting for him. Sometimes he would ask me to go through all but his personal correspondence and summarize what I could. I'm sure he thought this process would be educational for me—which it was. And at the age of fifteen, it also made me feel rather important! He was not biased against young people. He thought the more you learned about the world, the better."

The ranch was always home for my parents. No matter where they had been in the world, they were always anxious to return to South Texas. They loved being there, working, hunting, fishing, reading, writing, and sharing their lives with family, friends, and guests. As much as they loved Texas, they were citizens of the world, always searching for ways to nourish those who lived in regions with limited resources.

Daddy often said, "This is God's world, and we are the stewards of it." Both my parents built their lives on this belief, a belief that is the legacy of King Ranch—itself the fruit of the vision, inspiration, and hard work of generations of Kings, Klebergs, Campbells, and all who worked by their side.

(preceding pages)
154 From left: B. K. Johnson, Tom Armstrong, Dick Kleberg Jr., Bob Kleberg Jr., Mary Lewis Kleberg, and Helen K. Kleberg in the Santa Gertrudis swimming pool, 1944

(following pages)
155 Standing from left: Bobby Shelton, Mary Lewis Kleberg (Dick's wife), Dick Kleberg Jr., Lucy Armstrong, John and Etta Larkin Armstrong, Dr. Zachary Scott, Sally Kleberg (in blue), Helen C. Kleberg, Mrs. Scott, Barclay Armstrong (child), Tobin Armstrong, Katharine Armstrong (child), and Anne Armstrong. Seated from left: Lucy Armstrong Junior, Tommy Armstrong (in lap), Henrietta Armstrong, and Bob Kleberg Jr.

156 Bob Kleberg Jr. with grandchildren (from left) John, Helen, and Emory Alexander

157 The Alexander brood.

158 Bob Kleberg Jr. with grandson John Alexander at Norias

157

Endnotes

1. *Texas Live Stock Journal*, September 6, 1890.
2. Tom Lea, *The King Ranch* (2 vols., Boston: Little, Brown, 1957), Vol. I, p. 217.
3. Ibid., p. 307.
4. *Texas Live Stock Journal*, June 14, 1884.
5. "Cuero Bulletin," *Texas Live Stock Journal*, June 23, 1883.
6. Robert J. Kleberg II, letter to his parents, July 24, 1881.
7. Ibid.
8. John Henry Brown, *The Indian Wars and Pioneers of Texas* (Austin: State House Press, 1988 [L. E. Daniel, 1880]), p. 290.
9. Ibid., p.291.
10. Ibid.
11. Lea, *King Ranch*, Vol. II, p. 475.
12. Brown, *Indian Wars and Pioneers of Texas*, p. 294.
13. *Texas Live Stock Journal*, September 6, 1890.
14. *Texas Stock and Farm Journal* 18 (August 4, 1897).
15. Cattle Raisers Association of Texas, "Executive Committee Meets," Corpus Christi, Texas, December 12, 1916, p. 4.
16. "Texas Cowboys Ride Past Kleberg Bier in Last Salute to Cattle King," *Kingsville Record*, October 13, 1932.
17. "Mrs. R. J. Kleberg, Sr. Dies at Santa Gertrudis," *Corpus Christi Caller*, July 30, 1944.
18. Wallace E. Pratt, letter to Mr. J. Kleberg, Kingsville, Texas, January 28, 1965.
19. Lea, *King Ranch*, Vol. II, p. 612.
20. Certificate to become a citizen of the United States of North America, State of Kansas, June 3, 1868.
21. Philip P. Campbell, personal journal, February 20, 1872.
22. W. A. White, *Emporia (Kans.) Gazette*, June 1, 1941.
23. Philip P. Campbell, personal journal, undated, p. 64.
24. Philip P. Campbell, *Congressional Record*, January 31, 1906, p. 1832.
25. "P.P. Campbell Dies; Ex-Congressman," *New York Times*, May 27, 1941.
26. W. W. Graves, *History of Neosho County* (2 vols., St. Paul, Kansas: Journal Press, 1951), Vol. II, p. 635.
27. Robert J. Kleberg, "A Review of the Development of the Breed: Historical Data About the Origin of the Santa Gertrudis Breed." N.p.: 1967.
28. Ibid.
29. Ibid.
30. Ibid.
31. Ibid.
32. Ibid.
33. Ibid.
34. John Cypher, *Bob Kleberg and the King Ranch: A Worldwide Sea of Grass* (Austin: University of Texas Press, 1995), p. 94.
35. A. O. Rhoad and R. J. Kleberg Jr., "The Development of a Superior Family in the Quarter-Horse," *Heredity* 37, 8 (August 1946), p. 228.

36. Robert J. Kleberg Jr., "The Horse and His Place in Present Day Life," *Cattleman*, 1941, pp. 145–46.

37. Ibid., p. 2011.

38. "U.S. Cattleman's Wife Dobell Fan," *Australian Daily Telegraph*, August 4, 1962.

39. "King Ranch Photos on Exhibit," news release, National Cowboy Hall of Fame, Oklahoma City, Oklahoma, December 1975.

40. Toni Frissell, *The King Ranch, 1939–1944: A Photographic Essay* (Dobbs Ferry, New York: Morgan & Morgan, 1975).

41. *Toni Frissell, Photographs 1933–1967* (New York: Doubleday, in association with the Library of Congress, 1994), p. xxxv.

42. "Mr. Rogers Finds a Real Ranch and Real Cow Hands in Texas," Will Rogers to editor, *New York Times*, November 6, 1931.

43. "Along the Trail," *Cattleman*, January 1958.

44. *National Cathedral School*, alumnae section, 1924, 1925, 1926, 1930, 1931.

45. Lea, *King Ranch*, Vol. II, p. 506.

46. "Typical Texas Ranches Now Fast Disappearing," *Texas Stockman 25* (April 19, 1904), front page.

47. "King Ranch, Nation's Largest Ranch Property, is a Laboratory Beneficial to All," *South Texan*, December 1937.

48. Proceedings of the Fifty-fifth Annual Convention of the Texas and Southwestern Cattle Raisers Association, Corpus Christi, Texas, March 17–19, 1931, p. 48.

49. Edward L. Bowen, "The Running Horses of the Running W: Robert J. Kleberg Jr., Master of King Ranch," *Blood-Horse*, June 11, 1973, p. 2007.

50. "Dawn Play under L. Balaski . . .," *New York Herald Tribune*, June 3, 1937.

51. Edward L. Bowen, "The Heart of Assault," *Blood-Horse*, April 25, 1981, p. 2407.

52. Bowen, "Running Horses of the Running W," p. 2012.

53. Ibid., p. 2011.

54. Evelyn Warning, letter to E. B. Spiller, Secretary, Texas and Southwestern Cattle Raisers Association, Coliseum Building, Fort Worth, Texas, March 31, 1936.

55. Lowell H. Tash and J. M. Jones, "Phosphorus: Experiments Show This Mineral Essential to Greater Beef Production in South Texas," *Cattleman*, February 1947.

56. Report of Proceedings of the Seventh Annual Convention of the Texas and Southwestern Cattle Raisers Association, Fort Worth, Texas, March 18 and 19, 1947, p. 188.

57. Ibid., p. 191.

58. Robert C. Ruark, "Millions at Steak," *New York World-Telegram*, March 11, 1948.

59. Cypher, *Bob Kleberg and the King Ranch*, p. 75.

60. Tom Lea, *In the Crucible of the Sun* (Kingsville, Texas: King Ranch, 1974), p. 26.

61. Donovan Webster, "The Orinoco: Into the Heart of Venezuela," *National Geographic* 193, 4 (April 1998), p. 19.

62. Carroll Keach, editor, *Robstown Record*, May 12, 1955.

(following pages)
159 Helen C. Kleberg and Bob Kleberg Jr., circa 1960

Back Fly Sheet Cattle waiting to be shipped from King Ranch by rail, circa 1945